# Validation, Sabotage And Freedom

## *The Nature And Effect Of Money On Your Life, Your Relationships And The World*

Kathryn Colleen, PhD RMT

**Trend Factor Press**

Trend Factor Press, a division of Sparticle Concepts LLC
1530 P B Lane #M4819, Wichita Falls, TX 76302-2612
KathrynColleen.com



ISBN 978-1-7356943-0-6 (paperback, English)
ISBN 978-1-7356943-1-3 (ebook, English)
ISBN 978-1-7356943-2-0 (audiobook, English)

To contact the author, or to find more information, please visit KathrynColleen.com. Your thoughts and questions are welcomed.

Cover art by Kathryn Colleen, PhD RMT

# TABLE OF CONTENTS

## The Ugly Side



## Unpacking The Budget Baggage

**Support For Your Journey**

# Introduction

# Validation, Sabotage, and Freedom

The nature and effect of money has been a running theme in my life since day one. It's a simple concept. Money is just a medium for exchange. It is more flexible than a barter system. You can buy anything with money. But the reality of this simple idea is anything but simple. Money, as an extension of ourselves, reflects how we see ourselves and others. Money ruins some relationships and solidifies others. Money, whether the lack of it or the abundance of it, effects us deeply as individuals, within relationships, and across humanity.

In these writings, I want to explore this complexity with you. We will begin with the role money plays in your personal life, whether you lack it, have just enough, or more than enough. Then we will explore the effect of money on our relationships. Lastly, but certainly not least, we will explore the nature and effect of money on the global scale across communities and on humanity as a whole. I want to emphasize that this is all from my own unique perspective. This is only my opinion, based on my own life experience, and the observations of the people around me and humanity at large. My intention is to bring you face to face with your own thoughts, habits and baggage around money. If you can see your relationship with money plainly, you can decide if it is a healthy one for you and what, if anything, to do about it.

Although you may use these principles to build a better relationship with money, ultimately possibly leading to wealth, this book is not about how to get rich. There are tips and ideas that worked for me scattered throughout. You might use them, or not use them. You may decide to give your wealth away, but this book is not about framing money as bad. You will have to draw your own conclusions.

It's about recognizing the nature and effect of money on our lives at a personal level, on our relationships and on humanity at large both good and bad. From there, you can draw your own conclusions as may fit your own unique situation.

## Money Baggage

As you read, consider your own thoughts, feelings, impressions and baggage around money. Let's get those thoughts down on paper right now. Take a few minutes to answer the following questions for yourself.

- What is money to you? Is it good, bad or neutral?
- What are the major experiences you have had around money? What impressions did those experiences leave with you?
- What are the stories you tell yourself and others about money?
- Do you think you have too little, too much, or exactly the right amount?
- If you want more, why do you want more?
- If you think you have too much, why? Where is this guilt coming from?

- In your mind, how do you view others who have what you see as too little, or what you think is too much?
- Do you find yourself judging how other people spend or don't spend their money? Why? What in you feels threatened?

These questions can start to reveal your deeply held beliefs about money, and therefore, how it has shaped your life, your relationships and your world at large. As you read, continue to examine how these ideas make you feel and why. What beliefs are we triggering here? Where did you get those beliefs? Are they still right for you now?

## The Nature And Effect Of Money

Money reflects emotional value. We use it to soothe ourselves, to do good for others, to sabotage ourselves and others, and to live our truth. Money is an extension of ourselves, and as such, reflects how we see ourselves. Show me how your spend your money and I will tell you what developmental stage you are in.

Debt can breed unworthiness. Gambling can breed powerlessness. Wealth can breed freedom, guilt, arrogance and far reaching philanthropy. Money in relationships can lead to deeper connection and deeper fulfillment, or to manipulation, violence and even murder. The dichotomy is even more pronounced at the global level where we both deify and demonize the rich and poor alike. Massive good and massive evil all spring from the desire for money, the possession of money and the expenditure of money.

It is a complicated subject that weaves its way into our very identities, into our relationships, and our societies. Whether the nature and effect of money is good or bad is entirely dependent on your personal relationship with it. Over the course of this book, we will be exploring more about the nature and effect of money from all of these perspectives. Throughout these discussions, I will call out important questions for you to answer. I want to help you explore and understand your relationship with money, and evolve that relationship to a place where your money works for you in a positive way, offering freedom, fulfillment, growth, deeper relationships, and greater good.

# PART I

# THE PERSONAL SIDE OF MONEY

# Money As An Extension Of Ourselves

## Money Reflects Emotional Value

Money reflects the value that we inherently place on things at a personal level. For example, a diamond is just a pretty rock, but we pay enormous sums for them. Why? Because of the emotional and symbolic value that they have in our relationships. That all important ring represents commitment, future wealth, and social status. Think about how publicly we flaunt and discuss a beautiful engagement or wedding ring. Admit it, ladies. You want that big rock. Why? Because it makes us feel worthy. It makes us feel important. It makes us FEEL. And we would pay anything to feel that way.

Consider the following questions...

- What objects do you own that make you feel a certain way? List out each thing (jewelry, vehicles, your house, things on your shelves, clothes, cash itself, etc), and how it makes you feel.
- What else could make you feel that way?
- Are there activities, people or experiences that could make you feel that way?

Similarly, we overvalue the things that we already own. When you list something of yours for sale - a piece of furniture, a house, a vehicle - you will tend to overvalue it. This is called the Endowment Effect, a term coined by Richard Thayer, considered the first to deeply explore the idea. He suggests that to have something and then not have it, feels like loss and loss is painful. We, as humans, will do just about anything to avoid loss. And so we overvalue the object to soothe that sense of loss. When you sell something, and you ask yourself what it's worth, you are really asking yourself what it will take to make the loss of it feel OK.

For someone on the other end of this transaction, they are going from not having it, to having it, which is a position of gain. What are they willing to pay to feel the triumph of gain? The answer is: not nearly as much as you need to assuage the loss. Unless, of course, they attach emotional value to the thing. We won't pay big bucks for something that is just a thing, but we will pay anything for love, freedom, security, or worthiness.

But it's not all about loss. It's about the ownership of the thing. You chose this thing. When you bought it, you made a choice. And you crave validation for that choice. You want to be right in having chosen that. If nobody wants it, if it has lesser value, then maybe you were wrong to choose it in the first place. Ouch. Being wrong hurts too. Having your preferences called out as lesser feels like social rejection. Deep in our subconscious, social rejection equals death.

These objects represent ourselves, our history, our growth and a dozen other things. To undervalue the thing is to undervalue ourselves and our time on this earth. So we are compelled to overprice it, just because we want to be worthy and we want others to validate that worthiness.

Questions:

- Consider the objects that you listed in the last question.
- What do these things represent to you?
- What do they represent about you?
- Who are you without them?

Placing too much emphasis on the objects we own can lead to buying as an addiction as we seek meaning and worthiness in our lives. Buying to soothe yourself is nothing new. They call it retail therapy and we laugh and encourage it. Buying something new makes you feel temporarily alive, valued, appreciated and rich. But this temporary escape from your current reality soon wears off, leaving you feeling just as empty as before, if not more.

The credit card industry was built around your need to soothe yourself with things. And it is all too common. According to the Federal Reserve, the average US household had over $8,000 in credit card debt as of June 2019, accounting for over a TRILLION in credit card debt across the country. That is how desperate we are to feel safe and worthy.

Questions:

- What are you wanting to buy lately?
- What are you escaping?
- What emotion are you seeking to acquire?

- Why do you not feel alive, valued, appreciated, rich, etc already?
- What can you do to feel that way without derailing your finances?

As with most challenges, the cure for financial self-sabotage is connection. Financial self-sabotage involves yourself and your money so the key is to focus on these connections. That is, your connection to yourself and your connection to your money.

After considering the questions above, take some time to explore the cycle of human development. See which stage you are spending the most time in. Do the exercises to move yourself forward towards more complete connection to yourself and your money alike. These are all detailed in the book, *Purna Asatti*, and in my writings at KathrynColleen.com.

## Money Is An Extension Of Ourselves

Money is an extension of ourselves. We can use it to create change and improvements in our lives. We can also use it to detriment and sabotage ourselves. Spending and gambling to the point of addiction is far too common. But spending for the greater good has fantastic personal implications.

We use money, often, to create change and improvements in our lives. You can use money for food, clothing and shelter, but you can also use money to forward your career. You can pay tuition to learn new skills, get a new certification or a degree that will help you get your dream job, or a better income. You can use money to improve your health with a gym membership, assuming you actually use it. You can even buy healthier food, which is not always more expensive, but it can be.

Money well spent can bring you joy through entertainment, days at the spa or vacations to beautiful places. You might buy a trip to a spiritual retreat or personal development workshop that pays emotional and life changing dividends for years to come.

For as many ways as we might use money to improve ourselves and our lives, we can also use it to detriment and sabotage ourselves. We spend on any number of detrimental foods, drinks, and activities. We shop, eat, drink and otherwise distract ourselves from our pain and frustration. Sometimes we sabotage ourselves because we subconsciously believe that we deserve to suffer. Sometimes we sabotage ourselves as a byproduct of an unwillingness to face our reality. Either way, it is a form of avoiding the hard work of seeing your truth, and building the life you really want.

Spending as an addiction is an all too common extension of this denial and avoidance. Retail therapy, as they call it, is a great distraction from your current reality. Finding something to buy gives you a temporary dopamine hit. It feels good right now, but wears off quickly because your reality is still there and has not changed.

Spending, in this way, can become addictive. The debt piles up as you say to yourself that you, "just need this." But no one purchase seems to relieve the issue for long. The shame and unworthiness pile up alongside the purchases and it all drives you deeper into the sadness and frustration that started it in the first place. It's a vicious cycle. Stopping is best done all at once by cancelling and cutting up all those credit cards and operating cash-only for a good long while until you change the underlying problems in your reality.

Meanwhile, spending for the greater good, can be a therapy of its own. Studies have shown that spending the same amount of money on something to benefit someone else, has longer lasting positive effects on your mood and mindset, than spending that same amount on yourself for temporary enjoyment. Even spending just a little bit for someone else's benefit makes us feel wonderful. Paying for the person behind you in line at the coffee shop, or leaving an extra large tip to the waiter or waitress are just a couple of simple ideas.

In this way, spending just a fraction of your normal shopping bill on others, pays dividends to your psychology. It makes you feel kind, and worthy. It changes your view of yourself and others. And THAT is what changes your underlying reality. When you feel worthy, you will stop sabotaging yourself and start using your money to better yourself.

In all of these cases, money is an extension of ourselves, not a separate entity. Money goes where we tell it to go. It is no more sentient than a baseball, and no less dangerous when hurled in the wrong direction.

How are you using your money right now? How would you like to change that?

## Money Reflects How We See Ourselves

Ultimately, money reflects how we see ourselves. If you don't respect yourself, you will not respect your money. Lack of self respect and self love is often reflected in how you sabotage yourself and others with your money. Shopping too much, buying the wrong foods, going further into debt, gambling, and the like are all forms of self-sabotage rooted in specific feelings like unworthiness or powerlessness.

Show me where you put your money and I will tell you everything about your current stage and self-image.

Our spending patterns evolve with us. It begins with our first concepts of money. As children, we watch our parents buy things. We first realize that we can exchange money for things we want. As children, we want a lot of things and tend to spend on things that bring us instant gratification like candy, snacks, and toys. We don't think about the future. Eventually, we find larger, more expensive things that we want and the idea of saving up becomes formed in our minds.

But keep in mind here that we are, all this time, watching our parents spend like so-called adults. You didn't realize it at the time, but they were showing you how they felt about themselves. You may have witnessed shopping addiction, gambling, debt, or any number of detrimental behaviors and thought they were "normal", just because you saw them all the time. As we grow up, we each assume that what we are witnessing at home is what normal people do; what everyone does. We subconsciously model our own behavior and life choices around that.

Questions:

- Did your parents believe that debt is a tool, or otherwise a good thing, or just a normal thing, or a bad thing?
- Did you witness gambling addiction or spending addiction in your family?
- How did your parents spend their money or save their money?
- Do you see yourself repeating these patterns?

- What would you like to change?

The way we use our money directly reflects the emotions driving that use.

Debt reflects lacking or unworthiness. We go into debt via loans, credit cards or even borrowing from friends, because we want something, but we don't have enough money to buy it. We lack. We are not enough. Taking on the debt becomes a subconscious admission of our own personal lack. It breeds the same unworthiness that took it on.

Gambling reflects powerlessness. You might gamble on rare occasion on a vacation near some casino. You might try your hand just a bit for fun, expecting to lose and thinking of it as paying for entertainment. This is a perfectly healthy approach.

Even in this carefully guarded approach, however, you are experiencing powerlessness. For some, it is an exercise in feeling powerless so that you can experience it, and therefore process it. It can be fun to let go of control. It can even be good for you to see that you do not have control.

The problem comes when other factors in your reality have you feeling powerless. When the baseline of your reality feels powerless, you run the risk of gambling to the point of addiction. You feel powerless already. You gamble for the distraction of it. But gambling makes you feel even more powerless, especially as you lose to the house (which is inevitable). So you gamble even more. And the same style of viscous cycle that we saw in the shopping addiction shows up here again, except now that spiral of addiction is based on powerlessness. The powerlessness drives you to seek distraction, but the distraction makes you feel even more powerless.

Extreme debt becomes a combination of unworthiness and powerlessness. In the beginning, we are spending to assuage the unworthiness we feel. But the debt mounts up. As the debt gets higher, it reaches a point where you could never imagine paying it off. This adds powerlessness to the mix. So now we feel incredibly unworthy and powerless to change it. This leads to completely spiraling out of control OR resolving to change our lives completely.

Getting out of debt becomes part of the self improvement journey. In a moment of desperation, wanting something better for ourselves, we resolve to make it happen. We resolve to find a way out of debt because something in us is tired of feeling unworthy and tired of feeling powerless. We decide we are worth the journey of self improvement. And we are.

Getting out of debt is an integral part of self improvement. The two happen often at the same time. Why? Because as you improve yourself, you improve how you see yourself and how you think about yourself. In short, you come to love yourself. Then you cannot possibly continue to sabotage yourself in a financial way, or any other way.

The journey out of debt, however, is not nearly as easy as the journey in. Like all experiences, it changes us. The climb out makes us feel even more worthy and capable.

We see our own power to change our situation. We develop stronger will, and self-respect. In that time period, we develop the other parts of ourselves as well. This time, the spiral is heading UP, reinforcing self-respect, self-love and better money choices over and over.

Questions:

- How much debt do you have? List out all of your debts from car loans, personal loans and student loans to mortgages, layaway programs, and money you owe to family and friends.

- Now look at your monthly spending. What can you cut back on to pay off these debts? Cut back on everything and then cut back some more.

- What are you willing to give up to be free?

# Debt Freedom And Financial Contentment

## Being Debt Free

Getting out of debt is often part of the larger personal development journey. When you think about all the dreams and desires you could finance if you didn't have all of those payments, the motivation drives itself. So what is it like when you actually arrive? What is it like to be debt free?

You might think that reaching debt freedom is one big party. It certainly is cause to celebrate, and you should do that. But mentally and emotionally it takes a few months for the new normal to be fully internalized.

The first month that you do not have to send any payments to anyone is rather surreal. The mailbox seems terribly empty. You just don't really have bills. Yes, you might still have a rent or mortgage payment, and utilities to pay like water and electricity. But it's just so little, compared to what it used to be.

If you have been using Dave Ramsey's "debt snowball" method, then the last debt you paid off was the largest, and you were throwing a large percentage of your budget at it every month. And now.... and now you have all that cash for yourself.

You go a little nuts that first month. You have denied yourself anything and everything in the name of debt freedom for so long that you splurge a little, as you should. You should feel the reward of all your hard work. You take a month or two to enjoy it as the the reality of your new debt free life sets in.

Then you start to dream in earnest. Remember all those dreams and goals you wanted to finance? It's time to start allocating for them in your monthly spend plan. The feeling of placing your hard earned money toward something that really matters to you can only be described as purposeful bliss. It feels amazing. It feels like, for the first time in your adult life, you actually have your act together. You have a vision for the future and you are in charge of making it happen. You are working just as hard as you did before; maybe more. You are saving like a squirrel in Fall.

You are saving so vehemently, because almost guaranteed to be on your list of dreams is financial independence - the state of having enough money that you can live off of the investment interest for the rest of your life and never run out.

The ideal of never having to work again, or simply being able to work on whatever you want regardless of whether it pays, is key for the large majority of us. But along the road to financial independence is a stage I will call financial contentment.

## Financial Contentment

Financial contentment is a key step. We don't psychologically (or financially) go straight from realizing debt freedom to financial independence and a permanent vacation. Financial contentment is the stage where you are debt free and actively saving for your dreams. You can calculate how many months (or years) it will take you to reach financial independence. The path is clear and you are moving along smartly.

You might spend years to decades in this stage. Every month you are saving for your dreams and goals, and every month you have some fun money to play with. You might take regular vacations. They might be frugal or more elaborate. Life is good. You can afford your favorite foods, some eating out money, some nice date nights, and opportunities for your children or loved ones. You feel in control of your finances, your life and your destiny. You are content.

At this stage, you might find a reputable financial manager to invest your money and help it grow faster. You are also likely investing in retirement accounts. Or you might decide to be your own investment manager and choose your own investment products. Either way, this is a bit of a brave new world and it is dizzying at first. It requires an incredible amount of trust - in yourself or in your investment manager. Do your homework to make sure they, or you, are worth that level of trust.

The effect of this stage is an overall happier and less stressed you, leading to better marriages and better relationships between you and your children or family. You are probably more relaxed and happier at work and that leads to more professional opportunities and promotions. It's a wonderful stage to be in. You cruise along, tracking your goals each month. And then one day, it just happens. You hit that magic number... financial independence... and the effect on you changes yet again.

# Financial Independence

## YOUR Magic Number

What is financial independence? Financial independence, as we will define it here, means having enough money that you never have to work again if you don't want to work. That is how you will think about it at first, anyway.

You have worked so hard to get out of debt and save for your dreams that not working for a while sounds really nice. When you first reach financial independence, you are very likely to spend a little while not working, just vacationing and checking off your bucket list. But eventually, as Tim Ferriss notes in the *Four-Hour Workweek*, you get bored and existential questions drive you back to some kind of "work". It just won't feel like work. And it may not be paid. In fact you might pay to do it.

Before we go down that rabbit hole, let's define financial independence in the way that you, in your post-delirium state, will eventually settle on defining it. Financial independence is a number. It is a measure of your net worth. And that magic net worth number is the number at which you can live off of your money for the rest of your life, doing all the things you love to do, no matter long medical science allows you to live. This number is different for everyone, because different people prefer different lifestyles, and because different people prefer different types of investments for all that net worth.

So what is YOUR number? To calculate your magic number, start by daydreaming about your ideal lifestyle...

- You could live anywhere in the whole world. Where do you want to live? Maybe you have a dream location, or maybe you want to be a full time nomad, and live in a new place every month. Or maybe you want to be semi-nomadic and live in a specific set of 2-4 places that you rotate through... winter in one place, summer in another.

- What kind of housing do you want? Do you want a house or an apartment or an RV?

- How do you want your day to go? What do you do with your time?

- How often do want to eat out versus cook at home?

There are no rules here. Design the life you want and figure out what it would cost for a year of that lifestyle. Take that number and multiply it by 25. THAT is your magic number.

Why? It's an old rule of thumb, but a good one to start with. Many years ago, many smart people calculated that you could take 4% of your net worth each year to live on, and even in the worst of all stock market scenarios, you would never run out of money. You could argue that, if investments are doing well then you could take more. But that discussion is better left between you and your financial manager.

So if you need $5,000 per month to live happily, that is $60,000 per year. $60,000 times 25 is $1,500,000 (1.5 million). These numbers sound unachievable, until you get there. Then they still sound huge, and fun, and not quite real, and awesome.

So you can see that the less you need per month to enjoy life, the smaller that magic number is and the easier and faster it becomes to achieve it.

## The Real You

The nature and effect of financial independence, once achieved, is profound. You stop giving a f*ck what anyone thinks.

Before your financial independence, you depended on the kindness of your managers, customers, and so forth. Because you needed the money. Now that you don't need anything from anyone, you will find yourself much more ready to be YOU.

This is a time of discovering and expressing your true self. You might see a straight-laced corporate executive with a conformist haircut turn into a long haired, motorcycle riding, tattoo-sporting free spirit who spends his time helping charities and delighting sick children. You might see your old work colleague turn in that pant-suit and conformist makeup to become a flamboyant artist or peace guru (guilty on both counts!).

You see, the persona we craft for our work and career life, is rarely the whole story. We might take an authentic fraction of ourselves and show only that, in order to fit in and climb the corporate ladder. But what if you didn't need anyone's approval?

It's more than a matter of designing your preferred lifestyle. It's about being your full, 100% self.

- What would you wear, if you didn't care what anyone thought?
- How would you do your hair?
- Would you have tattoos or piercings?
- Unusual makeup or none at all?
- What do you really want to spend your time doing?
- What is your purpose here in this life? Can you live it?
- What do YOU want? Just YOU?

It's heady stuff. Many people go a little wild in the beginning. It is a fun stage of experimentation and finding self.

I bet you had no idea that your money and your expression of self were so closely tied. This is an amazing time to explore YOU, your purpose and what you really want from this life. This freedom of self expression would be impossible without your financial independence. The two are inextricably linked.

## Showing It Off Versus Hiding It

Most people who are financially independent do not choose to let anyone know. They live small. They might live in the same house they have always lived in. Or they might even downsize to a little apartment or condo, or even an RV. They might travel full time and seem to have just disappeared, popping up on social media sometimes to share a photo.

They don't drive flashy cars. And they probably don't wear the latest fashion. They are all around you, but I bet you can't spot them. This is for a couple of reasons.

First, while you are getting out of debt and saving for your dream life, you are not buying fancy clothes, houses, cars or anything else. All your money is going toward the cause of independence. When you finally get there, you like your less expensive clothes, house and car better than anything else you might buy. You forced a level of minimalism on yourself and now you like it.

But familiarity is not the only reason that the financially independent among us choose to keep a low profile. There is also a security issue. If people think you have money, they will want some of it. We will cover this in more depth later in how money affects relationships, and how large scale wealth affects security. But for now, even in this state of net worth in the 1+ million dollar range or so, you are often better off keeping your financial reality under the radar. Many decide that they are better off if their children, parents and other family are not aware. There is nothing like family coming around to manipulate you for cash. You are better off keeping it quiet.

# Large Scale Wealth

## The Dangers Of Comparison

If financial independence were not complicated enough, let's talk about large scale wealth. Wealth, in any amount, is comparative. In some societies, a thousand US dollars is a lot of money. In some others, it is not.

We previously defined financial independence as having enough money that you can live off of the interest it produces. That is, you have enough money that you do not need to work if you don't want to. Instead of you working for money, money works for you and produces an income that you can then use for your day to day life. Financial independence came with its own perks and challenges. At that stage you already have to take measures to preserve your net worth and keep it generally quiet.

Now let's explore what happens when financial independence turns to large scale wealth. Some large scale wealth is larger than others. We need some definitions.

In the western financial world there are three types of large scale wealth: High Net Worth, Very High Net Worth and Ultra

High Net Worth. To qualify for these groups in North America, as of 2020, you must have liquid assets (investable cash, not houses, cars, and other tangible stuff), in excess of $1 million, $5 million or $30 million USD respectively. This definition does change a bit from bank to bank, but it is generally used at these levels across the investment banking and startup investment world.

There are well over eighteen million such individuals in the United States as of 2020. It is not at all unusual. As an individual, this makes you a High Net Worth Individual (HNWI), a Very High Net Worth Individual (VHNWI), or an Ultra High Net Worth Individual (UHNWI). If you have more than $100,000 USD to invest but less than one million in assets you would be considered merely "affluent" or you might even be saddled with the somewhat derogatory sounding "sub-HNWI".

These terms come out of the investment banking and venture capital worlds because these are the people who want your cash for themselves. In other words, they are the wolves at your door and they have categorized their prey to optimize their approach.

But the comparison is not all on the side of those who would steward your precious capital. The psychology of large scale wealth is fascinating to observe. When the wealth is yours, you run the risk of believing that you are smarter than everyone else. Because... just look where you are! Look at all the money you have. You must have done everything right. You can do no wrong! You are brilliant! You start to perceive yourself at the top of a hierarchy based on net worth.

But as much as you may be looking down your nose at those unknowing fools with no money, you are feeling, at the same time, lesser than those with more money. Poor me, I am only worth a few million, but Jennifer down the street just made UHNWI status, and look at all these billionaires. I am nothing. The problem here is in tying your perceived intellect, or worse, your worth as a human being, to the total in your bank accounts.

When we are young, we see people with yachts and big parties, buying pricey bottles of champagne and we think they must be doing something right. We think they are smarter or better than us, or both.

These comparisons - the ones you draw between yourself and others, and the ones others draw between themselves and you, or between you and others, are all false.

Funny enough, as you reach increasing stages of wealth and have more time, you might also be working on your self development. And you will come to realize that you are worthy of love, regardless of money. You internalize the fact that your money is just an extension of you, not a measure of you. You realize that how you spend your money is an expression of your self-perception. And quite often this leads to setting up charity efforts, over yacht parties. Overall, you make different choices.

You can spot the "new" money a mile away by these mistakes of comparison. New money is hierarchical. It does not know the danger of its own flamboyance. It is holier than thou. New money wants to tell you how to live. It is smarter than everyone. Your high net worth might be "new" for quite a while.

Seasoned money, as I will call it, behaves differently. Seasoned money is quiet wealth. It does not assume to tell people who to vote for. Seasoned money is focused on giving back, appreciation, and some form of charity efforts.

Although individuals with seasoned money might live in a beautiful house (or several), they do not show it off. They avoid the headlines, in general. They understand the dangers inherent in their wealth and have taken steps to protect themselves. Living rather quietly is one such step. They might also have set up trusts, investments, wills and estates documents, nonprofit organizations and other means of ensuring their wealth is used and transferred in ways that make them feel purposeful and secure.

## More Money, More Problems

As we discuss high net worth, it might start to sound scary. To an extent, it is. Most people think that if you have money, then you will not have problems. You can simply solve your problems with cash. While money can solve a lot of problems, it creates new problems of its own. This is not to discourage you from building wealth. This is to inform you of the nature and effect that you might expect when you get there.

As you build wealth, moving from debt freedom, to affluence, to financial independence, to high net worth and beyond, you are trading one set of problems for another, better set of problems, each step of the way. For example, when you are saddled with debt, you might have problems making your mortgage payment or finding money for food. These are incredibly stressful problems.

Once you work your way out of debt and you are building wealth, you will have problems such as friends not understanding why you are not eating out, or driving around in a beat up car because you are so focused on hitting that magic number in your net worth. Further down the line, you may have problems with friends and family hitting you up for money and scammers at your door. Eventually you trade those issues in for the challenges of estate planning, tax planning, and setting up trusts and/or charitable foundations. Deciding which global problems to tackle is a much better problem than wondering how you will eat tomorrow.

In the realm of large scale wealth, tackling your new set of problems now requires a team of experts. Your first team will likely include an accountant to advise you on tax matters, a wealth manager to watch the markets and keep your investments profitable, and a wills and estates attorney to help you ensure your wealth ends up in the right hands after your death, through mechanisms like wills, trusts and other legal instruments.

The first time that you put together this team will seem like drinking out of a fire hose. Just finding a GOOD accountant, a good wealth manager and a good wills and estates attorney are hard enough. There is massive vulnerability in choosing poorly here. Pick the wrong people and your money will disappear faster than Houdini. Pick the RIGHT ones and your net worth will grow, protected and assured.

At first, you will be a deer in the headlights just tying to understand everything they are telling you and making all the decisions they will ask you to make. Once the initial set up is in place, these professionals can do their job largely without your involvement. And then it hits you... you have a TEAM. That is scary, actually. And a bit exciting. You are on a new level now and must rise to meet it.

Money has an interesting effect on character... it magnifies it. If you were an asshole when you were broke, you will be a massive asshole when you are wealthy. If you were kind, you will be a saint. Interestingly, YOUR wealth will have the same effect on OTHER people. If your kids were entitled and manipulative before, they really will be now. If your ex-spouse was... well, whatever they were that made them your ex.... that too will be magnified and they will all come. People you never even met will be accusing you of things that never happened.

At some point, whether you are showing off flamboyantly or not, word will get out that you have money, and people will come after it. All kinds of people... people you never even met, and your closest family. At that point you will add another one or two people to your team: lawyers. You will endure a phase where you are not only fighting off attacks from every angle, you are (if you're smart) using these lawyers to clean up any vulnerabilities you might have hanging out there from past mistakes, forging solid protective walls around you and your wealth to ensure no new vulnerabilities arise.

If you have not yet faced these kinds of attacks, lawyer up NOW to assess your vulnerabilities and prepare strategies to mitigate them while you still have time. Don't avoid this critical step.

If you enjoy travel, especially as an UHNWI, but even as a HNWI, you might also have a kidnapping problem. Kidnapping is a problem even for those who have a recognizable name, regardless of wealth, because a recognizable name makes your would-be kidnappers assume you are wealthy, even if you are not. Simply "looking" like you have more than average can be a risk. It pays to read up on strategies to avoid this.

The first, most obvious step is to not look like money. Dress casually, don't wear jewelry, and otherwise avoid designer labels. For some, depending on where you are traveling, you might choose to hire a security team. If you do, vet them carefully to make sure they are not easily paid off to assist the very kidnappers that you are avoiding.

At a minimum, use a fake name for all hotel registrations, dinner reservations, and car services. You might choose one name per trip and use that name at each of the hotels, restaurants and car services that you use. OR you might change your name for each service. OR you might change your name every day. If the car service uses the wrong name, don't get in the car.

In extreme circumstances, you might even take the approach of booking several hotels and rotating between them. Or you might just pick a safer place to travel. The point is to assess your security needs and act accordingly. A consultation with a security professional might be in order.

It is usually after such legal attacks, and a kidnapping threat or two, that the wealthy decide that quiet wealth is better than fame. They go underground for a while. They show off less. They might even move to another, more rural area. Who can blame them? When fame cannot be avoided, or even if it can, smart HNWIs are found keeping as low a profile as possible. Now you know why.

Questions...

- What can you handle yourself, and what do you need an expert to handle for you?
- What are your vulnerabilities?
- Are you even mildly famous?
- Do you look like money when you travel?
- Do you have any vindictive friends, family, or ex-lovers who might try to exploit you?
- Do you owe anything to anyone?
- Do you have any contracts or settlement agreements that you have not fully honored?

## Wealth Guilt And Giving It All Away

One surprising but widespread effect of large scale wealth is guilt. Yes. You can work hard and sacrifice for decades, be smart about your spending, amass financial independence and the coveted HNWI or VHNWI or even UHNWI status, and feel incredibly guilty about enjoying it.

When you reach financial independence, you are quite likely over the million dollar mark as well. You might have even done quite well in the business world, maybe had a successful exit, or otherwise came into high enough net worth that now you do not need to work if you don't want to work. This is the first of several problems that lead to guilt.

You take some vacations. You have some fun. You check off all the bucket list items. You don't feel guilty at first. That comes later when you hear about your friends and family struggling. You see people having a hard time. Then you realize that you never struggle anymore. You never worry about the rent or food. You can have the best healthcare, the best wine, and the best everything else. And you wonder why you. Why not them.

Once you get past the temptation to presume you are better than everyone else or smarter than everyone else, you really do wonder how you got so lucky. But it wasn't luck, you remind yourself. You worked hard for years, possibly decades. You sacrificed and saved and invested or you worked relentlessly to make that business profitable. You spend a little time reminding yourself that you EARNED this. Unless, of course, you just fell into all that wealth, which can happen. That only makes the guilt worse.

Regardless, that guilt is another force pushing you to not show off your wealth. You don't need to rub it in anyone's face. To some extent, you are right. When people are suffering, they don't care to hear you preaching from your luxurious ivory tower. But those who truly love you, actually do like to see you happy. The lesson there is to be happy, but don't lecture or preach. Yes, share your joy. But don't be blind to their suffering.

Your guilt is not just about having the best stuff, or not having worries about rent and food and medicine. Your guilt is also about TIME. You now have time. You can do anything you want.

Some HNWIs choose to keep working and nothing much changes. If you love your work, why not? But ask yourself...

- Are you working out of guilt?
- Are you working out of not knowing what else to do?
- Or are you working out of a true sense of purpose?

These are important questions. Your time here on this earth is limited and precious. You can choose to solve major world challenges, or you can choose to hike in the woods and nap in a hammock. But frankly, you get bored. After all the vacations and the bucket list, you are left with a need to feel purposeful. Your basic human nature needs to feel like what you spend your time on matters.

The combination of wealth guilt, and boredom, often leads HNWIs to the same ultimate end... give it away. Some give away their time, others give away their money. Some give away both. Some pledge that upon their death, it will all go to charity. One by one, they go through the same thought journey to choose a cause to champion; or two or three.

If they have some celebrity power, they can give that too. It's fascinating to see which causes each person chooses. They are wildly varied, but based on their own individual answers to the same thought experiments.

Let's try it now.... consider the following questions:

- What is the most important problem in the world today, as YOU personally see it?

- What one problem could you address that would make a lot of other problems irrelevant?

- What one problem could you address that would have the biggest impact? Or the biggest impact for the money?

- What is the most important problem to tackle right this minute, from an urgency perspective?

- What will matter most a hundred or a thousand years from now?

- Suppose you had a thousand, ten thousand, a hundred thousand, a million, ten million, a hundred million dollars to put toward this problem. How would you tackle it? What would you do, or what kind of solutions would you fund?

- What if you only had a month to make a difference? What if you had a year? Ten years? Fifty years? A hundred years?

It's a lot to think about, actually. As you research all the problems in the world, it can be overwhelming. But you will eventually settle on the one cause that you are personally most passionate about, and a path that allows you to help to the best of your particular ability, using all the skills and experience you have built over the years. Now, you feel purposeful and excited.

# PART II

# MONEY IN RELATIONSHIPS

# The Ugly Side

# Anger, Violence and Murder

There is nothing like money to ruin a relationship, leading to anger, violence and even murder. As of 2017, according to the United Nations Office On Drugs And Crime, there are about 464,000 people murdered each year globally, outside of armed conflict. That is, 464,000 individuals die through homicidal violence.

There are four main motives for murder: lust, love, loathing and loot... that is, money. According to the UN, 19% of all murders were due to organized crime. According to the FBI Uniform Crime Reporting Program, there are about 5 people per 100,000 population murdered in the United States yearly, and therefore about 1 per 100,000 people in the United States being murdered each year as part of organized crime, specifically. And the primary goal of organized crime is... money!

But the overwhelming majority of murders are committed by gangs in the quest for money, non-gang perpetrators who are in the process of committing a felony for money or property, and family or acquaintances who are arguing, often over money. There are plenty of murders committed over lust, love and hatred, but money seems to take top prize as the ultimate motivation.

As all crime is just a combination of opportunity meeting motive, you can see why violence over money is so common. But it's not all about murder. Money arguments between spouses, business partners, bosses and employees, and families expecting inheritance, lead to all manner of domestic and workplace violence. And that all begins with anger.

In 2017, The New York post reported that a little under half of couples fight about money, but that 60% did not like their partner's spending habits, citing them as too frivolous or too tight in their spending. That means at least ten percent of couples have underlying anger about money that never makes it to the surface. And that's just couples.

What about siblings that were expecting an inheritance from mom and dad and find out later that they are cut out of the will, or will receive a less than equal share? What about employees who feel they are due for a raise? Or a business partner who finds out that the other partner has been embezzling, and now the business is going under?

Why do we get so angry about money in our relationships? All anger is rooted in fear. Yes, all of it. So the real question is, what is it about money that makes us AFRAID?

Money is survival. Money is how we buy food, have a place to sleep, and shoes on our feet. If you feel like you don't have enough money, you are really saying that you fear for your own survival. Money then becomes the surrogate for survival itself. Now you can see why someone would kill for it, or at a minimum, get really upset over it.

Let's do a thought exercise. When you think about the concept of money, in general, how does it make you feel? Happy, sad, trapped, scared, worried, hopeful, joyous,...?

Your feelings about money tell you a lot about your relationship to money itself. But more than that, your feelings about money drive how it affects you in your relationships. If you always feel like you don't have enough, then you will feel angry when you partner buys something new, because it makes you feel even more threatened. If your partner has baggage from a financially controlling past relationship, they will take your anger as a threat and fight back with anger of their own. And now you are fighting about money again.

The key to not letting money spark fear, and therefore anger is to...

- Understand your feelings about money,
- Don't take it personally when bosses or family don't shower you with cash, and
- Make a spend plan together with your partner every month and stick to it like a contract.

We will get into monthly spend plans later, and how they can strengthen your relationships, leading to snuggles instead of fights. For now, just be aware that money is an emotional thing for a lot of people. It can lead to anger, violence and even murder. That's another reason to keep your wealth quiet, and to never be a human ATM for family members.

## Manipulation and Extortion

When someone you know wants money from you, but they are not willing to go so far as violence or murder, they may resort to manipulation and/or extortion. This is far more common than you think. Manipulation and extortion comes, from my own experience, in three varieties.

1. If you want a relationship with me, you'll have to pay.

2. I'll be nice to you until I get the money and then I will show my true self.

3. Pay up or else.

### If You Want A Relationship With Me, You'll Have To Pay

This is probably my favorite. In this scenario, the person in question only wants a relationship with you if you are sending them money. They may go so far as to threaten to cut off communication with you, if you are no longer funding their life. They might even say out loud that any relationship is predicated on you sending them money.

They assume that you really want a relationship with them. They assume that you would be heartbroken if they, in their infinite awesomeness, were not part of your life. They assume wrong.

I have seen this tried several times but I have never seen it work. Why? Because if you are demanding cash payment in exchange for a relationship, that does not make you awesome. It makes you an escort. Nobody wants to be associated with someone who would engage in extortion.

Trust me, if you give a mouse a cookie, it's going to expect to be on your payroll for the rest of its life. By offering this ultimatum, the family or friend in question is actually doing you a favor. They are offering you a door out of a tortured and miserable relationship. Take it. Just say no.

The person in question will be shocked to find that you are not desperately awaiting their call. This shift in power dynamic may actually heal the relationship and offer an opportunity for a healthy connection, in time.

## I'll Be Nice To You Until I Get The Money And Then I Will Show My True Self

There are times when you might fund a friend or family member for a one-time or short term thing like college, a wedding, surgery or other one-off expenses. It can feel wonderful to help out. You are really close, right? And then as soon as they cash the check, they turn against you, seemingly out of the blue. Or if you are lucky they might just ghost you, never to be heard from again.

What just happened here? Well, my gullible and well-meaning friend, you have been played. You have been manipulated. Remember that crime = opportunity + motive. Maybe they did actually use the money for what they said they would use the money for. You freely gave the money for that purpose. Or maybe they used the money for some other purpose.

That really stings, doesn't it? How could they do that to you? How could they manipulate you like that? What you really mean is how could they see you as so unworthy? So lesser? Such an object to be manipulated, and not as a human being with a heart and feelings?

Every person on this earth goes through developmental stages. It begins with separating ourselves from our experiences (Stage Two), then understanding our needs (Stage Three), and then understanding the needs of others. Until you understand that others have needs too (Stage Four), you will not develop the capacity for empathy, guilt and shame. Until you have the capacity for empathy, guilt and shame, people are just objects to be used for the fulfillment of your own needs.

THAT is how they could do that. And that is how they will do the same to others, given the opportunity, until time and experience evolves them. Now, you already see their mistake here. They can never come back to this bank again, because the trust in the relationship is forever broken. There will never be trust here again. And if there cannot be trust, there cannot be any kind of real connection. They have cashed in the relationship. They traded it for short term money and then burned the bridge. If they return, you would be suspicious at best. You certainly would not be fool enough to give them money again.

Although rejection and the realization that you have been played are painful, be thankful for the lesson. Be thankful that you had the opportunity to learn this expensive lesson. Ask yourself this...

- Can you think back on your interactions with them and see it now?
- Can you see how they were hiding something and you ignored it?
- Can you protect yourself in the future?

**Pay Up Or Else**

The third type of manipulation and extortion is just outright extortion. Pay up or else... or else I will tell your secrets. Or else I will hurt you or someone you care about. Hell, it works for the mafia. Why not the everyday citizen? This is actually a crime, but falls short of violence and opts instead for the THREAT of violence or damage to reputation, relationships or career.

If you have something to hide, you are vulnerable to this. Spy agencies and criminals alike bet you have something to hide. This kind of extortion, blackmail as it is called, is common for celebrities and those whose wealth is well known.

There may be a constant stream of people who will threaten to claim all kinds of things... that you had an affair with them, that you fathered their child, that you hit them, and so forth. If you have nothing to hide, don't give in. If you have something to hide, get a lawyer and some good advice and consider prosecuting them for blackmail. Keep in mind here, no secret is a secret for long, so prepare for the inevitability that your secret will get out. The best defense against blackmail is to not have any secrets at all. Don't do anything that you wouldn't want on the news.

But what if they threaten to harm your family, friends, pets, business or property? This is criminal extortion, so obviously the first step is to get the police involved and warn whomever they are threatening to harm. The perpetrators may be bluffing or they may actually do it. Let the authorities figure it out. Protect yourself. That is why so many UHNWIs have body guards.

The nature and effect of other people's money is fascinating. Money becomes a representation of survival, but also of control and power... power over other people. If one can satisfy the need to survive and the desire for power and control all at the same time, they will. This is the foundation of organized crime and the root of this type of extortion. Because crime happens when opportunity meets motive, and you cannot affect motive, you will have to affect opportunity. Don't give them the opportunity to threaten you.

# Control and Oppression

Even in what seems like a happy relationship, money can be a mechanism of control and oppression. There are many individuals who actively prefer to give up having anything to do with the finances, and are happy to trust their partner completely. We are not talk about them. What we are talking about is when one partner actively convinces the other partner that they are incapable, assumes absolute control of all the accounts, does not share information or planning with the other, and ultimately uses that control to oppress the other partner. It happens.

**You're No Good With Money**

It starts when your partner convinces you that you are no good with money. They will point out that check you bounced ten years ago, or remind you of some societal norm that people of your gender can't manage money, or some cultural rule that they should be the one in charge. Eventually, tired of feeling lesser, you drop the subject all together and leave it to them.

### Only I Can Have Access To The Money

Once your partner controls the money, then they have all the access passwords, and they know where all the accounts are. If you try to get involved again, just wanting to know the state of things, you meet resistance. At first, it is resistance out of convenience. They just don't have time to show you everything. That devolves to wondering why you care, and then reminding you that you wanted them to take over.

If your partner resists sharing your financial information with you, that should be a huge red flag. Transparency and honesty is key in any relationship, romantic or otherwise. If they are hiding the finances, there is a reason. That reason could be massive debt, gambling losses, or simply that they just don't want you to know.

### Here's An Allowance

To get you off their back, they will offer you an allowance. Here's some money you can control. It's like telling your toddler that they are entirely in charge of their dessert choice. You don't really care what they choose, but it makes them feel like they are in charge. The allowance makes you feel like you have some control. After all, you can do whatever you want with your allowance. Remember when you were a teenager? Did you get an allowance? Why? Because you were looking for independence and control and your parents were not yet ready to give it to you. You didn't have independence or control then, and you don't have it now.

**Do What I Say Or I'll Take The Money Away**

To borrow a harsh but accurate analogy... a mouse approaches a mouse trap. He does not know what it does. He only knows that there is cheese and the cheese is just sitting there for the taking. The mouse does not understand why the cheese is free. So he keeps coming back to enjoy the cheese. And all the while, the one in charge of the trap is prepared to snap the mouse's neck at any moment. I did warn you that it was harsh. But it's true.

The one who has absolute control over the money, can take it away at any moment, for any reason. Soon enough, just like in the good old teenage days, if you displease them, they take away your allowance. Do you see how this genius mechanism of control was put into place? Good. Now you can avoid it.

Now, just because you are clueless about your finances and your partner handles everything, does not mean they will turn into a control freak and start oppressing you. According to a 2019 survey by PolicyGenius.com, 16% of respondents "did not know core financial facts, including salary, debts, assets, credit scores, ... about their partner." Only 43% of couples manage their finances together. So there are plenty of people who have one spouse manage the money primarily, while the other can have access and awareness anytime they like. 5% of the people surveyed would like to leave their partner but feel they cannot to afford to do so. There we see the percent of persons under financial control and oppression (in my opinion).

Financial control and oppression includes a great deal of secrecy. According to that same survey, 12-13% have secret accounts or credit cards, 9% have a secret retirement account, and 6% have a secret will. Perhaps most interestingly, 7% have a secret life insurance policy on their partner. Hmmmm. Watch your back and keep your finances open and transparent. Honesty is always the best policy.

# Forcing Attachment

So far we have seen how money, or at least the representations we attach to it, can trigger murder, violence, anger, extortion, manipulation, oppression and control. Yikes! You might see by now that we are moving from the worst effects to the not-so-bad-but-should-still-be-avoided effects. Eventually, we will get to all the most positive and good effects of money. But we are not there yet. Stay with me. Let's look at how money is used within relationships to force attachment.

**Love Me For The Money**

It's the oldest idea in the book. If I have money and a flashy car, then I will be surrounded by lovers and then I will finally feel worthy. This is every guy who ever drove up in an expensive car and tried to talk to a woman walking down the sidewalk. There are plenty of partners willing to love you for the money. Gold diggers, sugar babies, mistresses, and kept men. They go by many names. But they are all willing to act like they love you to enjoy your money. In reality, they are loving your money through you. You are just kind of part of the deal, and that's fine for now.

Don't get me wrong. You can be wealthy, and still find real, unconditional love. It just depends on what aspect of yourself you choose to lead with. If you look for love by flaunting your intellect, you will attract someone for whom intellect is a priority. But if you are looking for love by flaunting your wealth, you will attract someone for whom wealth is the priority.

And let us not rush to judgement here. Maybe you don't want a love relationship right now. Maybe you just want to have fun. That's OK. But at the heart of it, if you are looking for companionship, it's because you are looking for acceptance, physical or otherwise.

Eventually, you may choose to seek a deeper, more fulfilling connection. When that time comes, the good news is that money-based relationships are quickly and easily severed. Easy come, easy go!

## You Have To Be Nice To Me Because I Give You Money

Sometimes money is not the foundation of the relationship, but is used as a means to force continued attachment later. For example, suppose that your parents gave you money for college. If you are mean to them, they are not likely to pay for your school anymore. You will feel compelled to continue to be nice and to have a positive relationship with them, even if they are not nice to you. Or even if they ARE nice to you.

There may be no thought of control here. But the subtle, even imagined threat of not having that cash can make you maintain relationships that you might otherwise allow to fade away. And it's not always cash. Suppose your friend provides free babysitting for you. That would cost a lot of money otherwise. It has big cash value. You may find yourself putting up with more than you should put up with, just to keep getting that free babysitting.

## Maybe If I Pay For Their Life, They Will Be Nice To Me

As humans, we want so much to be accepted, especially by family, be it parents or kids or cousins. All too often, I see people paying for someone else's expenses and it is clearly to try and keep them close. This is a little different than using the money for control. They are paying their expenses in hopes that they can remain a part of their lives. This is not the kind of emotional extortion that we talked about before.

In this case, the family members in question never asked for this money as a condition for the relationship. The payer just assumes that if they were not paying, their family member would not have any reason to come around. It is an issue rooted in unworthiness. The idea is that money is all you have to offer, as opposed to love, acceptance, advice, caring, compassion or other traits. It is the payer who feels unworthy and offers essentially to pay their family to hang around.

Not many people would say no to a free ride, so the situation is absolutely endless. What is worse, is that those family members are rarely very kind to the payer. The payer is often destitute in the end, and dependent on those very people to take care of them.

In each of these scenarios, using money to force attachment ultimately amplifies feelings of unworthiness, and resentment. Is it the money's fault? No. Remember that money is neither good or bad. It is just an extension of ourselves. We make choices about how to use it. When those choices are based on unworthiness, the result amplifies that unworthiness. When those choices are made in hate or anger, the result amplifies your hate or anger. As with all things, the root emotion is the key.

Questions...

- Who are you sending money to? Why? Dig deep for the true answer.
- Who are you taking money from? Is someone else paying your bills?
- What would these relationships be, if money was not involved?

# Social Spend Pressure

Even our best friends and closest family, with the best intentions, can pressure us to spend when we don't have any money available. Social spend pressure comes in many forms, from dating to weddings, divorce, mooching friends, office parties, fear of missing out, and public perception of wealth. Let's explore each one.

**Dating**

When you are dating, there is pressure to pay for your date's meal, or movie ticket, or whatever the date might entail. This pressure comes from a lot more than old fashioned ideas about who pays for what. Dating spend pressure comes from a place of simply trying to impress your date and endear them to you. For example, if you are the one who suggested the concert, there is pressure for you to be the one who buys the tickets.

Old fashioned ideas about who pays for what only complicate things further. If you are a man, you might feel pressure to pay, or you might think that a woman has expectations that you will pay. As a woman, you might be worried that if your date pays, they might expect something. So you might prefer to pay your own way, or really eliminate that issue by paying for the whole date yourself.

Bringing up the subject of money before the first date probably makes you both squirm. You just met and now you are supposed to make joint financial decisions? But if you would bring it up, you might avoid a lot of awkward pressure later. Or you can see how it all goes and decide at the end.

**Weddings**

Other people's weddings are a major source of social spending pressure. You want to give them a nice present, but their registry is full of expensive items. If you are in the party, you will also have to pony up for a suit or dress of their choosing, and possibly travel. And let's not forget the bachelor or bachelorette party. It can amount to a sizable expense.

The average person marries at a reasonably young age, when most of their friends are just starting out career-wise. Imagine that. You just got into the working world and now all of your friends are getting married seemingly all at once, piling up multiple major expenses in the same year or two.

**Divorce**

Divorces, later, have their own issues. Obviously divorce is financially devastating to those who are splitting up. There are few things on this planet that will kill your finances faster than a divorce. Alimony and child support eat into your monthly income while lawyer fees eat away your savings.

So, why do roughly half of all couples choose to put themselves through such an incredibly expensive and stressful challenge? Because it's worth it, as the joke goes. Yet for many couples, the expense of divorce alone keeps them together and miserable. That financial pressure works both ways.

**Mooching Friends**

We all have that friend. You know the one... the friend who always manages to have you pick up the tab at restaurants. Or the friend who always asks you to bring the expensive stuff to the party, while they bring the cheap stuff. Or maybe the friend who's down on their luck again and just needs to crash on your couch for a few days that somehow turn into weeks and months. But they are your friend. Maybe they have been your friend for a long time. You don't want them to be upset with you, so you keep paying.

### Friends In High Places

On the opposite end of the friend spectrum is the wealthy friend who expects you to keep up with their expensive tastes. For example, they may suggest you get together to catch up over dinner, and pick an expensive restaurant. Meanwhile, you are trying to get out of debt and save money. Maybe your income is much less than theirs. But they don't seem to notice.

This pressure comes from a friend who does not think about your financial situation. It could be that they are not aware of your situation. Or it could be that they just don't care. Often it is ignorance, not malice. In these situations, honesty is the best policy. A good friend would understand.

## Office Parties

Even the office can be a source of social spend pressure. Just when you think you came here to MAKE money, now you have to contribute to someone's birthday fund or the office pizza party. This is particularly frustrating when you are saving like a madman on the road to financial independence. The irony of your work being the thing that sets you back a bit from the goal of not having to work... it's diabolical. And yet, you cannot say no. You depend on this job. So you pay, and you feel powerless. The powerlessness is the worst part.

## Social Media

Even social media will put spend pressure on you, if you let it. Your friends are posting images of themselves with the latest and greatest and most expensive things. Now you have to have those things too. It's the modern version of "keeping up with the Jones's". You see your friends seemingly happy with their expensive new things, and it slowly eats away at your own feeling of worthiness. You wonder why you haven't "made it" yet like they have.

In reality, they may be neck deep in credit card debt over all of those flashy new things, and they might be miserable. But nobody talks about that on social media. We only show the filtered, photoshopped perfection that we want everyone to see. The problem is that you think it's real. And you think maybe that object would make you happy too. Spoiler: it doesn't.

**Public Wealth**

Lastly, what if YOU are the wealthy friend. When your wealth is public - either because you told everyone, or because your name got out there - people all of a sudden expect you to pay for things. More money, more problems, remember? Your friends and family may pressure you to spend. And your love for them may cause you to agree. It's a kind of emotional blackmail.

So what can you do? All social spend pressure has the same solution... boundaries. Simple policies and a monthly spend plan, along with radical honesty, solves each of these. If you cannot afford to do something, there is no shame in saying so out loud.

Having a blanket policy makes it easy to say no. For example, you might have a policy that you always pay your own way on dates, or that you only participate in one wedding party per year, or maybe you never allow friends to stay more than two nights. Individuals rarely feel slighted by a blanket policy that applies to everyone. It keeps it fair. And fair is key among family and friends. And with that, if you respect your spend plan, regretting honestly to your friends that you are out of going-out money this week but you can go out again next week, your friends will come to respect it too. Make a plan, set the policies, and be brutally honest about it all.

# Unpacking The Budget Baggage

The spend plan or monthly budget is the key to solving just about every money problem that could crop up in a committed relationship. Even for the individual, a monthly spend plan is critical. Sounds easy enough, right? Just sit down, list out your expenses and your income, and make a specific plan for where every dollar of that income will go. Cover your critical items first, then pay off your debts, then save for the future, and so forth. So why is it so amazingly difficult when you first try it? Baggage...

# Spend Plans Versus Budgets And Thog The Destroyer

Even the WORD budget might make you cringe. If so, change the word. Call it a spend plan. We all have baggage around these words. Budget sounds like a plan to restrict something, while spend plan sounds like you are planning to spend. And you are. Some of that spending might be on saving. The point is to call it whatever you want. Choose a word or phrase that makes this more enjoyable and helps to detach it from your past. If you have to, call your budget a pet name, like George, Betty, Fluffy, or Thog the Destroyer. Make it fun. It's hard to be too serious when you say, "Hey, babe, we should take sometime tonight with Thog The Destroyer."

## The Spendthrift Versus The Free Spirit

Within each couple, and within your own individual mind, is a battle between the desire to spend and the desire to save. Some people are naturally free spirits. Their nature is to spend and not track it too much; just go with the flow. Other people are naturally savers. They prefer to not spend and instead defer that joy to the future by saving up like a squirrel in Fall. They love a good spreadsheet.

The free spirit will say, "let's live NOW!", while the spendthrift urges, "let's save for our dreams!". Both are right. Sometimes you can have both of these archetypes within the same person, who likes to save but periodically has to bust out of the good behavior and splurge a little. This comes from a very human place. We have dreams and goals, but we recognize that life is short and we want to live now.

The spendthrift versus the free spirit is just one way this existential dilemma plays out in your finances. Remember, your money is just an extension of yourself. If you can balance the free spirit and the spendthrift, you will have the best of both worlds: A little fun money to spend any way you please, and some savings to forward your dreams.

Questions...

- What is your tendency? Are you the spendthrift or the free spirit? Maybe a bit of both?
- How can you allow for both living now and saving for the future?

## Letting Go Of Past Financial Relationship Baggage - I Am Not Them

Money is the source of the majority of fights in a couple, leaving lasting scars well into your single phase and beyond into your next relationship. If that is your history, then you have some baggage. Maybe they spent uncontrollably. Maybe they lied about money. Maybe they did not allow you to spend a dime.

Whatever the pattern was that caused friction and fights, your mind will expect that pattern to repeat again in your next relationship. If your last partner was too strict with money, you could be triggered by the mere suggestion of cutting back a little to save. If your last partner was a spendaholic, you could be triggered by a lack of tracking or accountability.

Here is the important perspective: your new partner is not your old partner, and you are not their old partner. That seems obvious, but your subconscious does not see it that way. If you find yourself getting worked up during budget meetings with your partner, try this...

Look at each other and say, out loud... "I am not ______ (insert the name of their past partner here). I am not going to hurt you like that. I love you." If you are single, you can look in the mirror and say it to yourself. Be very honest about your past experiences. Describe what you are afraid of repeating and build in plans to avoid it.

For example, if your past partner was too restrictive, build a line item in your spend plan and call it Fun Money. This is money that you each get to spend any way you want, no questions asked, no judgements given. Make it a number that everyone is happy with.

If your past partner was a wild spender, you might be afraid that your new partner might go off plan and spend too much. Pledge to each other that this spend plan is sacred. Fun money is your wiggle room to do what you want, outside of the plan. And that too is part of the plan.

In the beginning, check in every week to see how you are sticking to your plan, AND how you are feeling about it. Too restrictive? Not saving enough?

You are learning how to make choices and craft a plan that works for you as a couple (or as an individual). Eventually, your baggage will be unpacked and nonexistent. Consistency is key. Just keep working on it. You will find your groove within a few months.

## Getting On The Same Page

These techniques will get you to a point where you have a spend plan that is satisfactory for both of you. But satisfactory is not great. That's just passable. You want a spend plan that actually gets you excited. Yes... an exciting budget. Maybe even a sexy budget!

So how do you get there? The answer is shared vision. Tie your financial goals to your life goals.

- What would you do if you could do anything?
- What could you do if you were debt free?

Money is just an enabler of our dreams. It is the storm that brings the rainbow. Focus on the dream at the end of that rainbow. If you can create a shared dream - a vision for a life that excites you both - then the spend plan is your active mechanism moving you in that exciting direction. If your dream is filled with beautiful, romantic feelings like love and freedom, then yes, your spend plan becomes... dare I say it... sexy. Later we will discuss how you are building your relationship as you build your spend plan. For now, just craft a shared life vision and the financial situation to make it happen.

**The What-Are-You-Willing-To-Give-Up Game**

Spend plan meetings should be fun. So here's a game you can play. Inevitably, you will have something you want to save for. You will have some short term savings goals, like a new roof for the house or a new car, and you will have some long term savings goals like paying off debt or a nice vacation.

That means you will need to cut back in other areas, to have money for this goal. Take turns naming something you would be willing to give up, in the name of saving for this particular goal. "This goal is more important to me than ________." Consider them sacrifices to Thog The Destroyer, or whatever pet name you have chosen for your budget. See if you can one-up each other.

## The Courage To Get Weird

Cutting back on expenses to save for your dreams becomes somewhat addictive. You see your debts going down and your net worth going up and it's EXCITING. It's exciting because you feel the level of control that you now have over your own destiny.

First you cut back on the obvious stuff like eating out, and frivolous shopping. Then, if you can work up the courage, it's time to get weird.

- What is the one thing you THINK you can't do without?
- What if you tried doing without it for just one month?

For example, when we cut off the cable TV service to our home with three teenage boys, we expected an outright revolt. As it turns out, they didn't even notice. They had already figured out that online options were better. We saved money, and found a better way. Maybe you can find a better cell phone plan, or a better deal on groceries.

But don't stop there. You might decide to get rid of that expensive car with a monthly payment, opting instead for a cheap car that you paid for in cash. You might try not buying anything for a month or two or even for a year. You might get a side job, or start a business, or sell everything you own and move to Costa Rica where your expenses are next to nothing. Maybe you sell everything and become professional house sitters and live rent-free all over the world. That's a thing!

The point is this: don't let society dictate how you must live your life and what you must buy. YOU get to choose what car you drive, or whether you drive at all. YOU get to decide where you live and how you live. Get creative. Then get more creative, until you are downright weird. Then OWN it.

## The Spend Plan As A Contract

Your spend plan is a sacred document. It's that important. It is the mechanism of your life and dreams and should be treated as such. Whether you are single or in a couple, that spend plan is a CONTRACT.

That means you should have a dollar number above which you must change the plan. This is critical. You see, no plan survives contact with the enemy. Things come up. The unexpected seems to happen nearly every month. So along with your plan, you need a way to change the plan on the fly without derailing your dreams. If you need a five dollar part for your car, that may be no big deal, but what if you need something bigger?

For example, the hot tub breaks down and needs a new pump. Yikes. Pull up the spend plan for that month and decide what you are going to give up to make this happen, so you can still end up with a healthy savings at the end of the month.

You might decide that anything over $100 requires a quick spend plan adjustment. Or you might decide that anything over $10 requires an adjustment. Make it appropriate to your situation. Unexpected expenses will happen all the time. Never go off plan... update the plan instead, and stick to the new plan.

**Mutual Respect And Accountably**

I cannot stress this enough - trust is the foundation of any relationship - even with yourself. To sabotage your finances is to sabotage yourself and your relationship. Respect each other's fears, baggage, dreams and needs, and hold yourself and your partner accountable.

That means, neither one of you is the budget nazi. You both are. No one person should have to be the kill-joy. Mutual respect and accountability means that you both make sure that the budget plan takes care of everyone involved and you both make sure that you both stick to it.

We are all human. Sometimes your partner will be tempted to make an emotional purchase. It is up to you to stop them, with love and compassion. Can you find another way to handle the emotions behind this desire? Can you offer comfort, rebellion, or whatever they need, in some other way?

# Building Your Relationship As You Build Your Spend Plan

Money is never really about money. It's about emotions, and psychology, and dreams. Money, therefore, becomes yet another mechanism for building stronger and closer relationships. It starts with shared suffering. Wait, hear me out. When you first start getting your finances in order, you will be cutting back on expenses. This is an opportunity to get creative. In that shared experience, you will find deeper connection.

**Five Dollar Date Night**

One of my absolute favorite things to come out of our hard core saving phase was five dollar date night. We had cut every expense to the bone. NO eating out. NO concerts or movies. But dating your partner is incredibly important. You should never stop dating, romancing and getting to know your ever-evolving partner.

We decided to turn it into a challenge. You get five dollars. Not each... five dollars total. And.... go. We had to come up with date ideas that cost literally five dollars or less, gas included. And boy did we! A romantic walk to a beautiful sunset view, playing guitar in the park, long hikes, pic-nics with a tiny box of wine to share.

Without the distracting environment of restaurants and theaters, we had to pay attention to each other. We had the time and space to talk about deep things; to dream. These dates were infinitely more romantic and meaningful than the standard restaurant or movie date. We were present with each other. As a result of this "shared suffering," we were closer and all the more connected.

Even as an individual, cutting back on distraction-based outings and taking the cheaper nature-based options forces you to meet and connect with yourself and your truth.

**Trust And Reliability**

As the months go by, trust and reliability grow, from nothing more than the fact that you stuck to your spend plan. Even as an individual, you will come to respect yourself more for sticking to your plan. When your partner sticks to the plan, you see that you can trust their commitment to your shared dreams. You see beyond doubt that you can rely on them to keep you on track when you are tempted to stray. You can rely on them to be open and honest and a true PARTNER. And that all leads to...

**Better Sex More Often**

I could write a whole book on better sex through better connection; and I did. But for our purposes here, let's just sum up the the financial aspects. Better sex with your partner starts with trust, safety, and grounding. If any of these are lacking, your sex life will be lacking too.

You will come to find that your monthly spend plan meetings, as mundane and not sexy as they sound, are a foundation for trust, grounding and safety. This naturally leads to closer connection and that in turn leads to better sex more often.

But it doesn't end there. As part of your financial discussions, you have to express your dreams, be brutally honest about what you want and don't want, and stand strong in your own individual needs. These are all critical elements in a deeply connected relationship. Each one builds on the other to create nearly transcendent connection. And THAT translates first and immediately into the bedroom... or any other room.

Even when you are working your way out of debt; sometimes BECAUSE you are working your way out of debt, you will immediately notice how much more purposeful you feel, how much more bonded you feel and how much more often you feel in the mood for love. Enjoy.

# Dreams And The Magic Number

We have spoken before about the importance of having a dream that drives your financial engine. Psychologically, it makes the difference between staying on track and losing motivation completely. Your dream needs to be so emotionally compelling that you would sacrifice ANYTHING to make it happen...

# Dreaming And Saving

The art of dreaming comes down to asking yourself a series of questions, while holding off any negative voice that tells you it cannot be done. It can be done. We have seen a few of these questions before. Let's add to the list now and really get the creative ideas flowing.

In all of this, I am asking you to design a life that makes your soul sing...

- What do you really want to spend your time doing?
- What is your purpose here in this life? Can you live it?
- What do YOU want? Just YOU?
- If you could live anywhere in the world, where would you live? Why?
- What kind of home would you want to live in? A house? A hotel? A ship? An apartment? A treehouse? Urban, countryside, jungle, ocean, river or suburbs?

- What is your ideal daily routine? What activities, and outings do you like?

- What skills, degrees, languages or certifications have you always wanted?

- What is the biggest problem in the world today, as you see it?

- What would you do, if you had time, to help solve that problem?

- What is on your bucket list that you have not yet done?

Nothing is impossible. Even if something seems impossible, there is often a way to do it that you were just not aware of. For example, suppose that you would like to live in a big beautiful house in Tuscany with gardens and dogs. Maybe you can't afford to buy a big beautiful house in Tuscany. But you COULD become a professional house sitter, and work periodically in Tuscany where you will live rent free and enjoy that big beautiful house and gardens while you take care of the dogs and property. OR, what if you bought a house in Tuscany and rented part of it out as a vacation rental or bed and breakfast? You might actually find a new career and live your dream at the same time. Nothing is impossible. FIRST dream the dream. THEN find a way.

In terms of your relationships, you will want to make sure that your dreams include your personal dreams, your partner's dreams and some shared dreams too. Find a way to make it all work together. If you have small children, include them too. You may not need to put off your dreams until they are grown and gone. Read up on nomadic families who travel the world with their children in tow. Even if world travel is not your thing, it will show you just how many options there are.

## Your Magic Number For Financial Independence

We have spoken before about your magic number for financial independence. It will not be any different for a couple than for an individual, but we will get a little more detailed now.

Now that you can envision your dream life, chart out how much that would cost per year. Make an example spend plan as if you were living that life. What would it cost for rent, groceries, cell phones, all the outings you like to take, travel, and everything else. Research it! Go get actual prices. Really. Suppose you would like to live in Lisbon, Portugal. Look up menus for the kinds of places you would want to eat. Look up places to live and what they cost. Get in there and research real numbers and actually write up a monthly budget. It might be a lot smaller than you thought... or a lot larger. But now you have accurate numbers.

- Take your total for the month and multiply that by 12 to get your yearly budget. Keep in mind that this is after-tax money.

- Now take your yearly budget and multiply that by 1.34 to account for taxes. This is your pre-tax number.
- Take your pretax number and multiply that by 20 or 25. This is your magic number.

Once your liquid net worth (the sum of all your investments and bank accounts) hits that magic number, you can withdraw 4-5% per year for life and never run out of money. That 4-5% is exactly your yearly budget before taxes, leaving you at least what you need after taxes to live your dream life, and maybe more.

There is one big assumption here that you have INVESTED your net worth, rather than just stuck it in a savings account somewhere. You will be living off the interest it creates. That is, you no longer work for money. Money works for you.

Suppose you like a really simple life on the beach in Costa Rica. Maybe you need only about $2000 a month. That would be $24,000 per year before taxes. Multiply that by 1.34 and you get a yearly pre-tax need of $32,160. Multiply that by 25 and your magic number is: $804,000. Look at that! You don't even need to be a millionaire!

If you have more extravagant tastes, your number will be larger. That's OK. Your magic number is unique to the life you specifically want to live. Depending on your age and work history, things like pensions and social security can reduce that magic number even further by providing some of the monthly income you will need, without pulling from your investments.

# Financial Fatigue And Falling Off The Wagon

That magic number can look terribly large. If you are working your way out of debt, that magic number can look impossible. You cannot fathom being worth that much. And because it seems so very far away, you are in danger of financial fatigue.

Big dreams can take some time to materialize. Getting out of debt and saving for your dreams can be a years-long process. Meanwhile you are cutting expenses and sacrificing while you watch your friends take vacations and have fun... and pile up debt, but you don't get to see that part. It's exhausting.

Periodically, you may run out of steam and feel like it will never happen. That is when you fall of the wagon. You bust out and splurge on something. It may be something small, like overspending your eating-out budget. But it may be large like taking an expensive vacation. Either way, there may be regret.

It is important that you are compassionate with yourself when you fall off the wagon. It happens to all of us. Just climb back on and keep going. There will be plenty of setbacks along the way, and some of those setbacks will be you. To err is human.

To prevent financial fatigue and falling off the wagon, build some splurge money into your plan every now and again. If you splurge every month, it won't feel special. You need to play to your psychology here. Build in some splurge money every 3-6 months and enjoy it. That will make sure that when you do fall off the wagon, the damage will not be as bad.

## Loosening Up Once You Arrive

Once you reach the magic net worth you have been working so hard to achieve, it's not the major party you might think; at least not right away. You see, people have a really hard time switching from years of conditioned behavior to save and sacrifice, to immediately spending and enjoying. You will actually have to practice loosening up.

Start small and work your way up to whatever is appropriate. At this point, you don't need to save anymore, if you don't want to. You can have some fun with that money if you can convince yourself to allow it.

The first time you indulge in a spa day, it is going to feel really weird, like you don't belong. Indulge a little. Take care of yourself. Get some nice gadgets. Get your nails done. Have a nicer bottle of wine. And feel gratitude for it all. Look back to see how far you have come and how hard you worked to get here.

## Survivability

Lastly, once you arrive to that beautiful place of financial independence, you will need to put some thought into not messing it all up. Enlist the help of a good financial manager (see our past discussion about that). Part of their responsibility will be to make sure you don't ruin your new found financial freedom.

In your discussions with your financial manager, make sure you cover survivability. That is, when one of you passes away, how can you make sure that the other will be well taken care of? This is a financial issue and a wills and estates issue so you will want to talk to a good wills and estates attorney and get your paperwork up to date. If you have children, you will need to think about how you will want your wealth divided among them when it is all said and done. Welcome to HNWI status. You now have "people". Don't skimp on these vital team members. They will make sure you can enjoy your dream life worry free.

# Your Parents' Money

## The Chosen Child

Your parent's money doesn't seem like something that should be any of your business. And it's not any of your business.... until all of a sudden, it's your responsibility. Some of you will become your parents' keepers, physically and financially. Those of you who are the keepers will likely be the executors of their estate. And for some reason, this seems to completely blindside the grown children of aging parents.

Your parents might be in a financial bind, or they might be fine, or they might be wealthy. You don't really know until you ask. But rest assured, if you are the only child, or the "chosen child" - the child who will most likely be in charge of their care and will be executor of their will - you need to have some idea of their financial state and what the plan is.

Within any typical family, siblings all know who the chosen child is. Let's not pretend. Parents have favorites. In the instance when Mom favors one child and Dad favors another, the parent that survives the longest will determine the chosen child. So step one is to get your head out of the sand and recognize whether or not you are that child.

If you are not that child, you will play a much smaller role, but you will still want to be generally aware of the situation so that you can anticipate what may be asked of you by your siblings. The point is: don't go into this blindly as if they are going to be healthy and live forever.

# Awkward Conversations With Mom And Dad

It all starts with some very awkward conversations. Most parents don't like to discuss their finances with their children, especially if they are in debt, or otherwise struggling. It is an issue of pride. But it is also an issue of your parents not liking to think about their own future declining health and their own eventual death.

You don't need to have all the details right now, but you do need the basics, and you do need them to create an emergency notebook that DOES have all the details in it. If you are the chosen child, start a series of conversations in the safe and relaxed atmosphere of their home. Once you get the conversations rolling, and everyone is comfortable talking about it, you can move these discussions to phone or video chat as needed.

You want to AVOID coming across as the harbinger of death, or the money grubbing child just waiting for an inheritance. The easiest and best method I have seen to date for opening this conversation is to tell them about a friend of yours whose last parent recently passed, or was recently diagnosed with dementia, and the mess they went through trying to figure out where everything was, what was owed where, how to deal with all their parent's stuff, and so on. If you don't have such a friend, find an article about someone who went through that situation online and they can be your friend for the day. There are endless stories of chosen children being left to spend literally years to a decade working out the mess of their parents' finances and estate. Pick one.

After hearing what these folks went through, your parents may volunteer their plan as a means to soothe your worries... If they have a plan. If they don't volunteer a plan, you can ask... "We should have a plan. I want to be able to take care of you in the way you would want. Maybe now is a good time for you to write up what you would want me to do." This approach sets you up in the role of serving their preferences, as opposed to seeking your own gain or avoiding your own pain. If they need guidance in making their plan, a good wills and estates attorney can advise them on all the aspects to think about and plan for.

One thing the attorney may not cover is what I will call an emergency notebook. This might be a digital file, or an actual notebook. The emergency notebook should be stored with copies of the wills and estates documents, or at least with a copy of a power of attorney document to allow you to manage their finances and a letter of intent, directing you as to HOW you should handle the finances if they are incapacitated. The emergency notebook should contain...

- A list of where all their bank accounts and investment accounts are located

- Associated contact information for those banks and any investment managers

- A list of websites for those accounts and associated login credentials

In your ongoing conversations - this is not a one and done kind of talk - you should be sure to cover how they feel about long term care options, and what they would prefer.

# Supporting Your Parents Without Going Broke

In a 2020 survey, AARP found that a full one third of adults in their thirties and forties had sent money to their parents for things like groceries and housing in the last year, with half sending over a thousand and 20% sending over $5,000. These were not one time favors. These were weekly or monthly payments.

This is why it is so import to understand the basics of your parent's financial situation. First, you might be able to head off problems before they arise. If you can prevent them from ever being in a financial hardship, that is obviously best. If you can not prevent it, you might need to recommend and assist with things like selling their house, refinancing a mortgage, filing appropriate paperwork, and so forth to ease the situation. There is always something that can be done.

A common course of action is inviting your surviving parent, or parents to live with you. As of 2016, according to Pew Research, 20% of households were multigenerational. This actually marks a return to multigenerational living that in

1950 included 21% of households, but had bottomed out in 1980 at 12%. The driving factors are reported as economics, and secondarily as health issues. Most people do prefer independent living, hence the rise in popularity of assisted living facilities.

It makes sense to think ahead and coordinate with your parents about what plans would work for everyone involved, even if you are no where near ready to implement them. You DO NEED time to plan and save to avoid derailing your own financial situation.

## Unequal Distributions Among Siblings - You Are Not Entitled To Anything

The concept of inheritance can bring out the worst in everyone. Anytime money is being distributed, people are drawn back into Stage Three psychology, focused on their own needs, comparing themselves to each other, and comparison always ends in emotional turmoil.

Suppose you are the chosen child. You have spent years caring for your parents as your siblings gave little assistance. Maybe they lived in other states far away. It doesn't matter. From your perspective, you may feel that you deserve the majority, if not all, of any inheritance. Maybe your siblings, who just now showed up, feel that they deserve an equal share.

The reality is... and this is really important... YOU ARE NOT ENTITLED TO ANYTHING. You might have worked to take care of your parents for a decade only to find that you were left out of the will entirely. Don't be in this for the money. If you are the chosen child, and you accept that role, and you carry out that care, do it out of love.

Ultimately, your parents' wishes should be respected. However they declared that their estate should be given out, is what it should be; even if that means you get nothing. Assume you get nothing, and be pleasantly surprised if you get anything at all.

Besides, is that inheritance a blessing or a curse? Cash money is certainly a blessing that you could use wisely. But don't forget the taxes on that. Or maybe you inherited an entire HOUSE! But there's a mortgage and a bunch of repairs needed and it's full of stuff and now you will spend a year or more full time cleaning it out and selling it while trying to make the mortgage payments and maintain your own job and life at the same time. Maybe you would prefer to be written out of the will entirely.

# Your Children And Your Money

## The Typical Parent-Child Financial Journey

They say, you can have child, or you can have money, but you can't have both. Well, that's not exactly true, but children are, in fact, one of the most expensive things you will ever bring into your life. As of 2017, the average American will spend $233,610 to raise one child from birth to seventeen years old. (See the 2017 report from the U. S. department of Agriculture.) If you pay for college, that is even more money on top of that, potentially more then doubling your investment.

All that expense is made up of 29% housing, 18% food, 16% childcare and education, 15% transportation, 9% healthcare costs, 6% clothing and 7% on everything else. It comes to over $13,000 per year, per child. Obviously that goes up or down depending on where you live and how you live. Some parents pay much more, and some get away with less. Now factor in that the data for that survey was taken in 2015 and consider inflation rates. Yikes!

Inevitably, as you spend an average of over a thousand a month on your precious baby, they will not appreciate it. You will find yourself frustrated at how little they seem to understand money, what it takes to earn it, and how to spend it wisely. The typical path looks like this:

- You start them on an allowance and/or offer work around the house as a way to learn the value of money.
- You encourage them to get a job of some kind as they get a little older.
- Regardless, they always seem to be coming to you for money for other things. You become the perpetual ATM.
- Without good boundaries in place, you might fall into giving them everything, or keeping them on the payroll too long, ultimately stunting their independence and deteriorating your relationship.
- Recognizing your mistake, you make the fateful choice to cut the cord and kick them out of the proverbial financial nest (and possibly the actual nest).

- The relationship is strained at best during this transition to financial and therefore total independence, but soon flowers into an actual, real, deep and meaningful relationship on the other side.

# The Value Of Money

What do we mean by the "value of money?" As soon as we see our children waste money, we start using that phrase. "That kid doesn't know the value of money." Literally, the value of money is just the actual value. Five dollars is five dollars. What we really MEAN by the "value of money" is the work that it takes to get that money, and what you can then do with that money.

Allowances are typically the first method that parents use to teach their children about money. You give them some money each week or month and see if they can learn how to spend it well. According to the American Institute of Certified Public Accountants, in 2019, two thirds of parents gave their children an allowance at an average of $30 a week. Four out of five of those parents expect their children to do chores around the house to earn that money. Three quarters of parents in that survey said the allowance was to teach "financial responsibility" and the "value of money". But only 3% reported that their child did anything remotely responsible with it.

Have you tried this? How did that work out for you? If you are laughing right now, then you have truly learned the lessons of this phase of your financial life. They spend it on things that delight them, not on what you wish they would spend it on. They spend it, in short, on things that you would deem useless, frivolous, or wasteful.

You are certain that you have failed. You try to teach them better. They don't seem to get it. They need to save some! They need to research their purchases and not be so impulsive! They need to think about their future!

If you step back, you will see that you are expecting them, at all of eight to maybe eighteen years old, to act like a fifty year old financial expert. Deep down, you are expecting them to NOT remake the mistakes YOU made with money. That is what is really going on. You want them to do better than you did so that maybe life won't be so hard for them. Harsh but true.

Seeing that allowances didn't do the trick, you move on to encouraging actually working for money in the real world. Once they turn fifteen, they are eligible to work in most localities. State and country laws vary, so be sure to check the law in your area.

In a study by the Hamilton Project and Brookings Institution, we see that in 1979 a full 60% of teens aged 16-19 worked at least part of the school year. By 2019 that number was 35%. This is attributed in large part to increased homework, more AP and dual enrollment style classes and generally school becoming more competitive and work-intensive.

For those high schoolers who do work in the real world today, they find themselves quickly more mature than their counterparts. Their work life may significantly influence their friend set, as they opt for friends who understand what it is like to juggle work and school schedules, and deal with difficult customers.

You may find your relationship with them takes on a different feel as well. When they have their own money, and are not beholden to you for that money, you no longer have any real authority. This is actually a good thing. Breaking the power dynamic between you and your children, in this way, gives you an opportunity to let them practice financial independence while still under your roof.

They will not need an allowance. They can be responsible for their own fun money. You can stop being the perpetual ATM. The trade off is that you don't get any say in how they use that money. They might buy a phone or even a car. They might spend it frivolously. Or they might save it like a squirrel in Fall. Usually they do a little of all of those things.

This is a good time to let them make their own choices. If you are feeling the need to control their decisions, that is an indicator that YOU need to spend some time exploring your own need to control, not exacting authority over someone else's hard earned cash. You have to let them go... you might as well start now.

Rest assured that your children will make all manner of financial mistakes, and social mistakes, and career mistakes. We all do. They will find their way; some sooner and some later and some after great hardship, but they will find their way.

# Mom And Dad - The Perpetual ATM

As they find their way, and make their mistakes, they will have messes to clean up. As a parent, it is hard to watch them heading right for a train wreck and unable to do anything about it. You are Cassandra. You see the future and try to warn them, but they don't believe you. Or maybe you were not in the loop at all.

And now here they are. They failed to plan, they failed to save, or they failed to act. They may be faced with a surprise repair bill they did not see coming, or they are late on their regular bills, or seemingly down on their luck. They just need some cash this one time. And then another time. And maybe another time.

Each time they come to the Bank Of Mom And Dad, they are sad and distraught. You can't stand to see your baby suffer. You can't stand the conflict in your own heart. You want to help, but they need to learn. You are not sure exactly where your responsibility ends. It IS just this one time, after all.

Sometimes, you can help and not hurt, but sometimes your help is actually hurting them. For example, if they think they can always come to you for money, they will not save and prepare for potential disasters. If you take the safety net away, however, they will have their panic moment and might start saving for both the joys and disasters that lay ahead for them. When major disaster strikes, like a major medical problem or literal natural disaster, you can step in and help without it becoming a habit.

The difference is in the cause. If they caused their own mess, it is psychologically better for them to be the one who cleans it up. If they did not cause their own mess, you might choose to help. A cancer diagnosis or tornado that destroys their home is not their fault. You are not standing in the way of karma here. Helping in any way you can, financial or otherwise is a good idea and may strengthen your relationship.

Past due bills and unexpected repairs, however are the result of their failure to plan. If you step in there, you are preventing life from teaching them the lessons they so desperately need. As a result, your relationship will suffer.

So why does the relationship suffer? When you clean up their messes, you stunt their independence. Subconsciously, they may resent you for it. I have seen parents who continue to pay for their grown children's cell phones and rents, only to have their children repeatedly insult them at every opportunity. When independence is stunted, maturity is delayed. Your relationship with your children is meant to evolve, not stagnate. The result of paying for their life or cleaning up their messes, beyond a certain age, is a grown man or woman acting like a thirteen year old.

Each of us on this earth wants to be free, independent and capable. That skill is not inherent. We have to learn to be free, independent and capable by getting it wrong enough to know how to then get it right. In short, they have to make their own mistakes and you should let them. Yes, it is painful to watch. Stay out of it anyway.

So why do parents do this? Why do we pay for too many things, for too long? Why do we keep cleaning up their messes? The answer is personal to each of us, but the most common causes are guilt and unworthiness. YOUR guilt and unworthiness, to be precise.

Divorce is a common cause of guilt leading to financial disfunction with your kids. Divorce, your own childhood experiences, your current marriage and other factors can also lead to feelings of unworthiness. In feeling unworthy of love, you might attempt to buy your children's love, subconsciously convinced that if there is no financial dependence then they would have no reason to love you.

In these situations, it is not your child that needs adjustment... it is YOU. Because it is not at all about the money. Isn't that always the case? Work to let go of your guilt and unworthiness. You are worthy. They are OK. You have nothing to be guilty about.

The relationship possibilities with a fully independent child are so much greater than than you realize. For now, suffice it to say that no relationship can be pure when money is involved. Let this tether between you drop away, and foster a deeper and more pure connection that will reward you both.

## Cutting The Cord

When you are ready to cut the financial cord, you can gradually step your kids towards independence, or you can end it all at once. The older they are, the faster you will want to help them find their feet. If you can start your kids on a path to financial independence early, you can step them down one bit at a time.

For example, they can get a job when they turn fifteen or sixteen. Once they have some income of their own, you can stop giving them an allowance. They can start paying for their own fun. By eighteen they can cover their own car insurance, cell phone plan, and everything else. Imagine that!

The maturity your children will gain by being financially independent from you will astound you. This kind of early and gradual method is just one way. Some parents like to step their children down to their own financial responsibility during the college years, or shortly thereafter. But the longer you wait, the harder it will be, and the further they will have to go to catch up in maturity. There is something about paying your own bills that makes you grow up quickly.

But suppose that you find yourself in the situation where you are paying your grown child's bills. Suppose they are done with school and somehow still on your payroll. They might even live with you. The psychological and financial effect of this arrangement is detrimental to both of you.

Apparently, however, you are in good company. In a 2013 study by Pew Research Center, we see that more than a third of middle aged parents were providing the primary means of support for their kids and it was not because they were in school. It can get really out of hand, delaying or outright preventing your own financial independence or retirement plans.

When it comes down to it, you might have to rip the bandaid off and stop supporting them completely in one fell swoop. In this case, when they have overstayed their welcome, the best solution is a clear deadline to be on their own. Set a reasonable expectation. It might be one month, or two, or even three months. But don't let it drag on.

Make it clear that this situation is costing you your future, and costing them their future too. Help them outline the steps to independence. Help them find a room to rent somewhere.

Help them find jobs in their industry. Help them learn how to grocery shop, budget and clean. Make it clear that you will always be there to coach them, but you cannot fund their life anymore. Express your confidence in their own ability to manage their life. And stick to your stated deadlines.

As the deadline approaches, they will take more action. They may also give you a lot of grief. You see, getting on your own for the first time is scary. It's terrifying, really. This abject fear of being on their own will cause some friction in your relationship as you approach each major deadline. Hold firm, and be kind. Simply refuse to engage in any conflict with your child. Be a fountain of peace and joy... a fountain with clear iron-clad deadlines... and love.

Reward each step towards independence. Celebrate getting a job, getting their own space, taking over their own bills, and so forth. Treat them as the adult they are becoming: independent and capable. In many ways they will be looking to you to tell them they are capable of all of this. If you are confident in their ability to be on their own, then they will be confident too.

After a successful launch, your relationship will change. It will go from parent-child to something more peer to peer. You will become a coach or mentor they can call on for advice as needed. The complete lack of any financial expectation in your relationship leaves it open, loving and pure. They call because they want to. They visit because they want to spend time with you. It is a more pure and more enjoyable relationship than the money-driven one you have now.

## Boomerangs And The Entitled

Sometimes, your successfully launched child comes boomeranging back into your home and/or your bank account. This can happen many ways. A major illness with a long recovery, or unexpected layoffs, can lead a once independent grown child to fall back into dependence. Layoffs are not really a great excuse but long term medical recovery is a hard one to say no to.

Having been independent, they might resent needing your help again. In these cases, clear boundaries and timelines will help everyone involved avoid the feelings of resentment and unworthiness that are common in this situation. Keep it clear and temporary.

Sometimes, instead of physically returning, your child might simply attempt to manipulate you for money from afar. I can imagine your shock at the thought. You precious baby would never lie to you or take advantage of you! ... or they might.

Look, not everyone on this plant is a nice person. Some people are assholes. And one of those assholes might be your child. It's not your fault. They are who they are, making the mistakes that they need to make and reaping the consequences.

It is entirely possible that your sweet, precious angel may lie to you, claiming that they need money for some really great cause, and then use it for something else. They might be particularly nice to you, or guilt you into giving them money for an actual need, and then turn around and be down right mean to you once they get the money. This too is manipulation. Chalk it up to an expensive lesson... for YOU.

The lesson is this: no relationship is pure or fully truthful when money is involved.

## Planning For The Inevitable

Just as you must plan for the inevitability of your parents' passing, you must also plan for the inevitability of your own. The only certainties in this life are death and taxes and they both require financial planning. Planning for your own exit from this world can be such a morbid task.

According to a 2017 study by Caring.com, only 40% of American adults had a will or a living trust. That number jumps to 81% of those over the age of 72. But that means 9% of Americans over 72 years old don't have any plan at all.

The average life expectancy in the United States is 78. But that does not guarantee you will make it that far. Having no plan will leave your children in a mess of probate court dates and paperwork that will not have them thinking of you fondly. A 2018 survey by EstateExec found that the average estate takes 16 months, 570 hours, $12.4 thousand dollars in legal and accounting fees to settle, and is worth $50,000-$250,000.

Even more pertinent is that 44% of all families devolved into conflict during this time. Most of that conflict looks like children and grandchildren fighting over inheritance, or one person getting greedy, misappropriating items or spending cash before the will can be read. There is nothing like money to really reveal a family member's true character. You might avoid sending your family into this type of conflict by:

- Making sure your wills and estates documents are solid and unquestionable,
- Naming an executor who will not inherit anything, but will instead be paid a fee for their effort, and possibly...
- Making your inheritance plans clear to everyone involved.

You might also consider distributing the majority of your estate while you are still alive. For example, if you want your house to go to your oldest child, and your vacation home to your second child, you might sign over the deeds to them sooner rather than later. Or you might simply add their names to the deeds, making it easier to transfer later. Consult a good wills and estates attorney in your locality about that.

What you should NOT do is avoid the issue. You WILL pass away someday. You need a plan. Think ahead about how you want your money and other assets to be distributed and get a good attorney to write it up correctly. That will include some hard choices, such as who will be in charge of your finances if you are incapacitated.

It's a vulnerable position to be in. It comes down often to a question of which of your kids is best with money. You can see the conflict brewing already! Leave very specific and clear guidelines for how you want everything handled. If all your kids know what you would want, they will keep the chosen child honest.

# No Relationship Can Be Pure When Money Is Involved

Ultimately, the nature and effect of money on relationships can be a positive one for couples but a negative one for family. Money among friends and family creates a power balance that subordinates one party below the other through dependence. This leads to altered behavior. That is, the dependent party will naturally choose not to reveal the full truth of their thoughts and daily lives.

Withheld truth means withheld connection. It can also mean lies, manipulation and misery. But at a minimum, it means you don't know them as well as you think you do and you are not as deeply connected as you could be.

**Power Balance**

When one person gives money to another, power within the relationship shifts to the payer. They who have the gold make the rules. There is a natural subordination that happens. You might tell yourself that you can take this money from your parents and not feel subordinate to them, but the reality is that you will indeed feel, even subconsciously, lesser, or in some way beholden to them.

You may withhold certain details of your life that they might not like, in order to keep in their good graces. It is the same way at work. Do you tell your boss every detail of your thoughts and your life? I doubt it. As an employee, you are more likely to show just those parts of yourself that promote the persona you need at work to get ahead.

You show part of your truth, not all of it. Sometimes you withhold a bit of information about yourself because you think it might get you fired or otherwise risk your income. Sometimes you just want your coworkers to like you. But the fact is that the money you get from working there causes you to show only part of your authentic self... specifically the parts your boss would prefer to see.

**Altered Behavior**

The person receiving the money will not share their full truth, out of subconscious fear of the money stopping. And THAT is an invitation to lies, manipulation, misery, and withheld connection. If you are desperate enough, your picking and choosing about what to show and what to hide could devolve into making up new facts about yourself, or even manipulating others into believing whatever benefits you.

You might even alter your behavior to please others to the point that you no longer recognize yourself. All of these situations lead to misery for you and everyone else involved. So what can you do?...

**Remove The Money, Open The Connection**

We see that the nature and effect of money on relationships is so much more than a topic to agree upon. The ripple effects of money pervade the very foundation of every relationship in your life... until you take the money out of the equation.

True independence opens the door to true honesty and therefore true connection. It doesn't guarantee it, but it offers the opportunity for a deeper and more pure relationship. The more financially, physically and emotionally independent someone is from you, the closer your relationship can be. That's why you may find you are closer to some of your friends than you are to your family.

Fostering this kind of complete independence with your parents, your children and everyone else, you can then enjoy a more complete connection with them all, if you choose to. Complete connection comes from expressing your full truth and seeking to understand their full truth. Once money is no longer a factor, your full truth can be shared and therefore understood and connection is deepened. Remove the money, open the connection.

# PART III

# MONEY IN THE WORLD

# Deities And Demons - Other People's Money

Other people's money is the stuff of headlines and neighborhood gossip. You can be assured that if people think you have money, some will deify you for it, some will demonize you and others will try to scam you out of it...

# Scammers, Con Artists And Thieves

According to the Federal Trade Commission (FTC), nearly $1.5 Billion was lost to fraud in 2018 alone. The most common forms of fraud were scams, fake debt collectors and identity theft. You might think that it's only the little old grandma that gets scammed out of money but the truth is that three times as many people in their 20s lose money than people in their 70s.

The young and inexperienced fall prey to scams more often but for relatively less money - an average of $400 per event, while those in their 70s lose an average of $750 per fraudulent event, but far less often. It is possible that older individuals are simply less likely to report the fraud, and more likely to just take the lesson and move on. Or it could be that younger individuals are more likely to be active online, exposing themselves to more scams.

Overall, according to the FTC in 2017, about 16% of the American population were victims of fraud. That means, of you and your six closest friends, one of you is going be taken advantage of financially, in the next year. Will it be you?

It pays to take steps to protect yourself from the basics like identity theft and credit card skimmers at the local gas station. For the grey areas of everything else, your best bet is to be skeptical and verify everything before you trust anything or anyone. For example, don't ever give out your personal data over the phone, or by text or email, unless you know with absolute certainty who you are transmitting it to and why.

Anyone can claim to be anything. You have to become a more skeptical person. To begin any interaction with distrust is unpleasant. But these are the times we live in. That includes looking out for unauthorized billing, as well as all those text based scams and phone scams you have come to know and "love".

Of course, if they cannot scam you out of it, they might just take it. It is a near certainty that your favorite credit card or debit card will be compromised at some point in the near future. One strategy is to simply assume that it will be compromised, and have a back up plan.

For example, have a second card for a different account handy so that you can cancel the compromised card and still operate normally while the first card is replaced. Then, when the second card is compromised, return to the first account which now has a new card. Wash, rinse and repeat.

## Deifying And Demonizing The Wealthy

We look up to the wealthy. We track them in popular culture as celebrities. I bet you can name your favorite billionaire... and your most hated billionaire. It's quite divisive, actually.

We see other people's wealth and make assumptions. We assume they must be smarter than the rest of us. Or we might assume they must be devious and evil. Ultimately, we are trying to understand how they ended up with these resources and we didn't.

We rarely assume it was blind luck. But often it was. Timing is everything. The right idea at the right time makes for a great business, regardless of who is in charge. But we don't like to think of our lives as being driven by chance.

Some billionaires are truly brilliant business strategists. Others just kind of fell into it. And some might have used untoward business practices to get there. We see each one of them as a deity to be followed and mimicked or as a demon to be lashed out against.

We rarely see them as human... which they all are... every one of them. They are just people. They are not deities. They are not demons. They are somewhere between, just like anyone else. They are imperfect, just like that person you see in the mirror each day.

We demonize the wealthy as a way to justify our own lack of wealth. If the wealthy are evil, we do not want to be evil. Therefore, we don't want to be wealthy. We convince ourselves that wealth is bad so it's a good thing we are swimming in debt, or just getting by.

But deifying the wealthy can have the same self-oppressive result. When you deify a billionaire, you are creating a large separation between you and them. You essentially say that they are wealthy because they are particularly special in a way that you could never be. It could never be YOU. The result is the same. You never try to improve your financial situation.

Consider the following questions:

- What wealthy individuals do you deify? Which do you demonize? Why?

- Are you using these mental gymnastics to justify keeping yourself in debt?
- How do you feel about wealthy individuals in general? Why? Dig for the truth in your past experiences.

## Neighborhood Jealousy

In all the discussions of demonizing and deifying the wealthy above, you were probably visualizing famous billionaires and celebrities. But what about the wealthier people in your own neighborhood? In every neighborhood, in every country around the world, some are better off financially than others.

When I was young, my parents sent me to a private school, because the school I was zoned for was famous for near weekly gang violence. My parents were upper middle class, if compared to the nation, but at this school we were the "poor kids". Within our own small neighborhood, we were average. It's all relative.

But what jealousy prevails when someone you know gets a shiny new car, takes an exotic vacation or appears to otherwise have wealth beyond the rest of you in the neighborhood. Within that microcosm, they are the wealthy, wether they are or not... it's all perception. They might be neck deep in debt for that car or that vacation, but they APPEAR to be wealthier than everyone else.

This comparative perception of wealth will drive their own neighbors to demonize them. Some neighbors will speculate as to what evil means they used to get such wealth. It's all jealousy. Their perceived MORE, makes you feel LESSER. And it is this feeling of being lesser that you don't like.

Note how, in all of this comparison, wealth is used as the basis for self-worth. We can measure our self-worth any way we like. We might measure ourselves by our education, or by our accomplishments, by how many books we have read, or by how many people we have helped along the way. We could measure ourselves by the goodness of our hearts, or the strength of our bodies. But we don't. We too often use money as a measure of our entire being.

- How do you measure yourself?

- How else could you measure your successes in this life?

- How else could you measure your "goodness" or "worthiness"?

## Millionaire Incognito

So you can see why the wealthy might lay low. Suppose you were a millionaire. Suppose you were a HNWI, VHNWI, or an UHNWI. Would you show it off? Knowing that you risk almost certain demonization, you would probably keep it to yourself.

You might have a nice house, but not so much nicer than your neighbors. You might take exotic vacations, but not tell many people about it. You might have a nice car, but keep it in the garage and take it out only occasionally. In other words, you would keep your wealth quiet, for the most part, in order to not be targeted.

Of course, it is not just to avoid being targeted. One does not accumulate high net worth by spending it. Many people have high incomes, but low net worth. If you spend all your income on houses, cars and other status items, you are not investing it and making it work for you.

So the majority of millionaires are actually found living in middle class neighborhoods, driving older cars and wearing inexpensive clothes. They invest their income. Their money is in diversified accounts and under the watchful eye of wealth managers, not sitting in their driveway.

There are several wonderful perks to being the incognito millionaire. First, you are rarely the target of jealous neighbors and family members. If people think you don't have anything, they won't come after you. Second, you have the peace of mind that comes from knowing you never have to work, if you don't want to. You are less stressed. When you choose to work, you work with passion and confidence, two things that always lead to success.

So is your seemingly nondescript neighbor actually a millionaire? Maybe. But they are smart enough to keep it to themselves. Maybe a more important question is:

- What are YOU doing with YOUR income to generate wealth?
- What could you do for society if you had a certain level of wealth?
- Where are you spending, when you could be saving and investing?

- WHY are you spending? What feeling are you seeking in all that spending? How else could you feel that way without spending?

- How much of your income could you save and invest, if you were really motivated?

# The Stick And The Carrot - Government Money

Governments use money in two ways, to encourage behavior and to discourage behavior. Follow me here. Your income is taxed. Your purchases are taxed. You are even taxed when you die. And all of that money that used to be yours now flows into government coffers at all levels: town, county, state and national.

Then what happens? The various levels of government use that money in three ways. They buy things like equipment and construction projects, they give cash to individuals and organizations, and they pay employees to collect taxes from you for other activities you might choose to undertake.

Each of these actions is a way for your government to encourage or discourage certain behaviors in you, your neighbors, and indeed other countries and individuals worldwide. It's not just about what your government does, it's about the EFFECT of what your government does. Let's take each in turn...

## Government Spending

Governments buy things. They buy all kinds of things. Local governments buy buildings and vehicles, road construction and office supplies. They pay employees to manage it all. National governments buy all of that plus military equipment, ships, planes, and everything else you can imagine.

When governments buy things, they spend large amounts of money. That spending creates entire industries just to provide the products and services that your government wants to buy. It encourages people to create those specific products and services that the government is paying for right now. The offer of money for specific products, causes more businesses to start making those products, to get that money.

The effect of government spending is an increase in those industries that make that stuff or provide those services. This also discourages businesses from producing products and services that the Government is not interested in right now.

There is a ripple effect. If the government chooses to buy several large military ships, new shipbuilding companies will spring up. They will hire lots of architects, engineers, electricians, plumbers, welders, security specialists and so forth. Seeing the demand in the job force, more young people will then choose careers as architects, engineers, electricians, plumbers, welders, and security specialists. Now the nation will have a larger number of people with that specific expertise. By buying a few ships, your government has just shaped the career choices of a generation.

Even if it is not about the money, government spending can affect behavior. Governments buy impressive military equipment more often to deter, than to start wars. Having a strong military capability deters would-be attackers. So buying that impressive ship has the effect of both encouraging ship building and the associated technologies and careers, as well as discouraging other nations from attacking or engaging in warlike rhetoric.

This then encourages fruitful trade negotiations and mutual aid pacts. These trade deals then benefit specific industries and products, which then encourages individuals and businesses to flock to those industries and make those products, which drives hiring and therefore educational choices all over again, now on a global scale.

But spending alone is not enough to fully guide individuals and businesses to do and make what your government wants you to do and make. That is where cheap loans, grants, tax breaks and new taxes come in.

# Loans, Grants And Tax Breaks - A Government's Way Of Encouraging Your Behavior

Many governments have programs that offer low interest or no interest loans, or grants for certain types of individuals and/or business activities. For example, if you, as an individual, meet certain demographic criteria, you might be eligible for a low interest business loan. If you are a veteran in the United States, you may be eligible for special mortgage options. If your business makes the right kind of products or offers the right kind of services, you might be eligible for a grant. This is the government's way of encouraging specific individuals to start specific types of businesses, or to buy property.

Tax breaks are an effective incentive as well. If you get a tax break for installing more efficient windows in your home, you might just do it. If your business gets a tax break for its marketing efforts, you are more likely to market more often.

There are tax breaks for all kinds of things. Once you know what they are, you cannot help but be drawn to alter your behavior accordingly.

Likewise, if you do NOT get a tax break for some activity, like meals and entertainment for your business, you are less likely to do it. That leads us to how governments use taxes to discourage behavior.

## Taxes - A Government's Way Of Discouraging Your Behavior

The more something costs, the less likely you are to buy it, right? Therefore, one way to discourage people from buying something is to tax it more heavily than other products. For example, when the United States government wanted to discourage people from smoking, they simply increased the taxes on cigarettes to the point that most people chose to quit, or to smoke less, just because of the cost. There was also a widespread advertising campaign. But the cost is what really got their attention.

Ultimately, taxes contributed to a change in public behavior. Want people to drive less? Increase taxes on gasoline. Want people to earn less? Increase taxes on larger incomes. You get the idea. Whatever you tax more, people will choose less. That includes products, services, and even their own income.

If you increase property taxes, people will choose to not own property. For example, in some localities, you pay a tax every year or every six months for the privilege of owning a vehicle.

Just the fact that you own it, means you have to pay money to the local government every year.

Let's pick on Loudoun County, Virginia in the United States, just because I have personal experience with that county. As of 2020, the yearly amount you owe is based on the value and age of the car. If you own a nice expensive new car, your taxes will be high. If you own an old car, or a cheap car, your taxes will be low. If you own a car that is more than 25 years old, your taxes will be zero.

So what do you think people will choose? They choose the antique car first, or an older or cheaper car next. The luxury car or new car is the least popular, although still widely chosen by those too wealthy to care. Overall, however, behavior within the county was shaped by the car tax structure.

Consider the following questions:

- What choices have you made recently, that were influenced by taxes and tax rates?

- How has government spending affected your career choices?
- How have tax breaks affected your choices within your home or business?
- What would you have chosen in each of these cases, if taxes and other government efforts were not a factor?

The way in which your government uses money affects so many aspects of your life. Consider that last question carefully... what would you have chosen, if you had not been influenced by your government? Would you have chosen differently?

# Stock Markets, Geoarbitrage And Philanthropy

# Money In Motion - Stock Markets & The Collective Mood

First, a disclaimer... I am not a stock expert. I am not giving you financial advice or investment advice. I am just telling you what I have personally noticed.

There are approximately 144 stock exchanges around the world. The largest is, as you might guess, the New York Stock Exchange (NYSE). The concept of stock is simple enough. A share of stock is a small piece of ownership in a company. If you really like a particular company's products or services, you might bet on their future success by buying some shares of stock.

That's how it should work, right? But the reality is so much more complicated. If you look at stock charts, what you see there is just the price per share. The price per share goes up and down over time. When you look at a chart of the famous DOW Jones Industrial Average or the S&P 500, you are looking at the combined price of a specific set of stocks, and how that combined price goes up and down over time.

So what drives it up? And what drives it down? Stock traders are always trying to dissect exactly those questions. Obviously, if a company is not making enough profit, that will drive it down. If that same company reports more profits than expected, that will drive its stock price up.

But it is so much more complicated than that. Headlines involving the company leadership, news about new government tariffs, or trade wars, new trade deals at the national level, and other local and global economic factors drive the price per share up, and down and cause all manner of volatility. That is why the charts look the way they do.

Stock charts end up looking like Brownian motion - totally random. Stock traders then use dozens of different measurements and indicators to analyze these seemingly random charts. When certain indicators say "buy", they buy. When other indicators say "sell", they sell. But it becomes a very emotional game.

When you watch the price of your stock drop, you are itching to get out of it. And that might be the wrong answer entirely. What if it rebounds?

Enter the robots. In a bid to remove the emotions and complexity from the stock market game, many traders prefer to use trading robots. These bots are just software apps designed to trigger buy and sell orders based on various indicators and measurements. Sounds like a great idea, until the average Joe gets involved. Since the advent of online trading, anyone can be a stock trader. And that means there are lots of people buying and selling based on emotion.

The result looks something like this: riots break out in some random city, nowhere near Company A. Media headlines, hungry for clicks, exaggerate and sensationalize the day's events. Emotional traders, fearing a total national crisis, start selling everything. The price of Company A's stock starts dropping, triggering a cascade of bots to sell, sell, sell.

Meanwhile, none of these traders has considered the question of whether Company A is actually affected by any of this. Or is Company A, instead, going to have an advantage now because of the day's events?

A few smart investors will do the research and spot a bargain. They will buy up Company A's stock and wait for the rest of the world to come to their senses. The crisis passes,

Company A's stock rebounds, and a few smart people just made a profit while a lot of emotional people and bots lost big.

The stock market does not trade by itself. It is not some nebulous electronic deity, or third party beast to be studied and predicted. It is just a bunch of people making choices about buying and selling. Some of those choices are emotional, rather than based on reality. So what you really see when you look at a stock market chart is this: human emotion.

In general, when people are upset, it goes down. When people are happy, it goes up. Negatively charged emotional happenings like civil unrest, national elections, and mass violence generally send stock prices down. Positively charged emotional happenings, like renewed stability, new trade deals, lower taxes, and peace agreements, generally send stock prices up. There are plenty of individual stocks that will not follow those trends, but in general, if you are watching the large indexes, this is what you will notice.

Fear will cause people to sell, which drives the stock price down, which makes other people afraid, which makes them sell too, and on down we go. Fear begets loss, and loss begets fear. Likewise, joy begets gain, and gain begets joy. So the nature and effect of the stock market's natural waves of joy and fear is this game we call trading. It is a magnified mirror of our own collective societal mood.

So what does that mean for you? Get a good wealth manger or investment advisor who is not emotional, but understands how emotions drive the markets, and don't freak out when the market drops. That just means it is in sale. Look for the bargains.

# Greener Pastures - Geoarbitrage

People, since the dawn of the barter system, have always looked for the best deal. Businesses seek the best employees for the least salary, and the best materials for the least cost.

Hundreds of years ago, transportation was just not what it is today. All business was local. People rarely moved. If you had a business, you had to source your employees, materials and products within a relatively small region. It was the same for the average household. You would source your food and other supplies locally.

As time moved on, however, transportation became faster and cheaper. Businesses and individuals alike could source products, materials and even employees from all over the country. This put the clothing manufacturer in Massachusetts in direct competition with the clothing manufacturer in Texas. It brought produce from California into the grocery stores in Florida and vice versa.

The "economic operating area" of each business had grown to encompass the entire country. That meant that your business or household could now find cheaper and better options from around the country. But that also meant that you as a business and you as an individual potential employee were now in competition with every other business and every other potential employee in the country. It's a double edged sword.

Enter the age of the internet. As the internet matured, so did communications systems, and transportation networks. Now here we find ourselves with global scale opportunities, global scale sources of materials and supplies, global access to talent and, therefore, global scale competition.

This is the essence of "geoarbitrage." This handy word simply means finding a better deal for your money somewhere else in the world. You might find a better deal on the manufacturing materials you need in the next state over, or in a country on the other side of the world. You might find that star employee in the same town, or you might have them work from another country.

Geoarbitrage benefits any location that can offer more for less. And that has put some localities at a particular disadvantage. Such is the nature of competition. But this is not new. For decades already, companies have moved from one state to another for cheaper operating costs and cheaper employees. Now those moves are global.

Governments around the world, recognizing that they cannot compete as well, place tariffs (essentially a tax) on certain materials and products entering the country, to try and level the playing field. Sometimes it works. But the trend itself appears to be unstoppable.

Take just the one subject of employees. If you have employees in the United States, you will pay taxes on the salaries that you pay them. But what if the kind of work you do could be done from anywhere? You could hire someone who is better educated for one quarter of the cost, have them working from another country, and not pay any taxes on their salary at all. That is a hard bargain to turn down. And THAT is the harsh reality... it is also the good news.

The nature and effect of this geoarbitrage is that you, as an individual in the western world, must develop more unique skills to stand out and be worth your higher, western salary. But you also have an incredible amount of opportunity in that you can afford to start businesses for a lot less money by getting help from around the world. And you can sell to the whole world as well.

That means niche products and services have a large enough market to be successful, while generic products become commodities, driving the prices too low to be profitable to western manufacturers. The effect, ultimately, is a plethora of niche products and services based in countries with a higher cost of living, and a plethora of cheap everyday products based in countries with a lower cost of living. For example, think about the products and services that you use. Your accountant or tax advisor is probably in your own country, but your clothes were made in another country where rent and food are cheaper.

But geoarbitrage is not just for businesses. At some point, you might say to yourself... wouldn't it be neat if I could have my western sized income, but a lower cost of living in another country? What if my rent and food costs were a lot lower, but my salary was the same? If your job is the kind of job that you can do from anywhere, you can make that dream a reality.

In Tim Ferriss's book, The Four Hour Work Week, he details some specific strategies for getting your employer to agree to remote work, and then moving yourself to anywhere you like, either temporarily or permanently. You might also start a business and design that business to be remote from day one.

Personal geoarbitrage does not necessarily have to be global. You might work for a company in San Francisco where rent - and salaries - are high, while living in rural Wyoming, paying next to nothing in rent. It's the best of both worlds; high salaries and low costs of living... lots of income and very little expense.

Once you get used to that idea, you might wonder just how low you can go with your expenses. Changing locations is just the first move. The more stuff you have, the more it takes to maintain it, store it and move it. The bigger your house, the more you pay in rent or mortgage, property taxes, heating and cooling, maintenance, and so forth. More stuff will necessitate a larger house, or paying for a storage unit. Eventually, you see that less stuff means fewer expenses.

That leads us to the idea of "going liquid." That means giving away or selling your possessions for a more minimalist or nomadic lifestyle. If everything you have can fit in a an RV, a suitcase or even a backpack, then your expenses might be very small indeed. Some simply choose to be this minimal. Others choose a nomadic lifestyle on top of this minimalism; or rather enabled by this minimalism.

When you can pick up and move to another town at a moment's notice, you have the flexibility to truly minimize expenses and continually place yourself in whatever location offers the best deal, or the most excitement, or both. As of 2018, The RV Industry Association reported that approximately one million Americans live full time in their RVs. Most of them work in some form. Thanks to advances in mobile communications, this nomadic lifestyle is incredibly feasible, depending on your type of work.

But of course, if you don't need to work, it is even easier. Remember our discussion about your magic number? If your expenses are this minimal, you would not need much net worth to never have to work again. For example, if you can live on $2,000 USD per month, then just $804,000 would keep you in a monthly income of $2,000 for life (using the 4% rule).

The point is this: your stuff or your freedom. The fewer material possessions you have, the more you can take advantage of geoarbitrage to optimize your lifestyle and your income, and minimize your expenses. That being said, your ideal life might be in one stable location with all your favorite stuff and that's fine too. Choose that location wisely.

Questions...

- If you could live anywhere, where would you live and why?
- Can you work remotely?
- If you were to start a business, what kind of business would you start?
- Could you design your business to operate entirely online?

## Feeling Good Versus Doing Good - Charity And Philanthropy

So far, we have discussed the nature and effect of government money on society, the nature and effect of other people's money on society, and the nature and effect of people on the stock market, and the stock market on people. Now let's take a look at the nature and effect of your own personal money on the world at large.

There are more than 1.5 million nonprofit organizations in the United States alone, as of 2019, according to the National Center For Charitable Statistics (NCCS). This includes all manner of nonprofit organizations such as public charities, civic leagues and chambers of commerce.

According to charitynavigator.org, in 2017, "An estimated $410.02 billion was given to charitable causes. For the third year in a row, total giving reached record levels." Wow! That's a lot of money. Over the past few years alone, well over a TRILLION dollars have been spent in charitable causes tackling everything from poverty, malaria, and lack of clean water to education initiatives and political reform.

People give money to charitable efforts for a number of reasons. Some give because they are focused on the mission of that organization. In turn, they feel like a good person, morally, for supporting something they feel is important. Similarly, some give because they like the tax break. In turn, they feel smart for reducing their tax bill by doing some good at the same time. Others give because their faith says they should. Again, they then feel like they are on the moral high ground.

In all of these cases, giving to others causes us to feel good, mentally and physically. It activates pleasure and reward centers in the brain, releasing dopamine. Check out research by the Univeristy of Oregon on that subject. Ultimately, all of these reasons boil down to feeling good about ourselves. Yikes. That is not what you expected, was it?

What about people who are out there volunteering and working for charities? Well, that is a slightly different story. Those who give of their time and effort still enjoy a shot of dopamine and the feeling of being a good person. But they also get to see the end result up close.

For example, those volunteers who actually hand food to the hungry or install a wood stove into someone's home or place a mosquito net around a bed in a malaria- vulnerable area, see first hand the smiles of those they serve, and the ripple effect of their efforts within that community. In this way, giving your time and effort towards a cause you care deeply about, is orders of magnitude more satisfying. But there it is again... personal satisfaction.

This dopamine reaction to giving money or time to charitable causes is what keeps donation numbers going up every year. It is quite literally addictive. That's great! So we might expect donations to charities to keep going up over time.

Now here is the hard question... Why do these problems persist? Why is it that we, as a collective humanity can throw over a trillion dollars at these problems and not have solved them? Because money alone is not the answer.

If throwing more money at the problem worked, over a trillion dollars in the last three years would have solved something. But of course, SOME good has come of it all. The question becomes, where and how are our charitable efforts actually EFFECTIVE?

According to GiveWell.org, the list of most effective charities in the world today are dominated by initiatives to distribute mosquito netting and vaccinations. These represent the most lives saved per dollar. But that is just one way to measure effectiveness. Saving lives is not always the goal. Sometimes the goal is increasing literacy or rehabilitating prison inmates.

One particularly clever charity example is Puppies Behind Bars. This charity solves two seemingly different problems simultaneously by training prison inmates to raise service dogs for wounded veterans and other uses. The inmates learn new skills and feel purposeful, reducing the percent that end up back in jail, and wounded veterans get much needed service dogs. These kind of local, niche efforts are often the most successful, but rarely publicized.

There are towns all over with small neighborhood level efforts providing lunches for local homeless children by sneaking food into their backpacks at school, businesses using pay it forward strategies to offer free food and drinks to first responders and those in need, small church mission groups adopting villages in other countries and actually flying there with wood stoves and installing them, and every other kind of effort you can think of. These are just examples that I personally saw first hand in the small town of Purcellville, Virginia inside the richest county in the nation.

But you don't have to go to the richest county in the nation to find great local charity ideas. When I was growing up, we would spend every Christmas with my dad's parents in the small, rural town of Oakman, Alabama. It was steel mill and strip mining country back then. Each year, my grandparents would adopt a family in need and bring them a Christmas tree, food of all kinds, toys for the kids and everything else to make for a well fed and happy holiday. My sister and I would tag along sometimes. My grandparents would get to know the family, make several visits and encourage them in their goals. They were always making real connections with everyone, from the poorest to the richest and everyone between, and they treated them all the same.

None of these efforts were publicized. They were led by everyday people who spotted a need and decided to solve it with their own effort and a little money from others... but mostly their own effort.

These small scale, local efforts, championed by everyday local people are capable of major impact. Why? Because locals know what the town needs. Locals know what the problems really are. Locals are passionate about their hometowns and about helping the people they are personally connected with. And why wouldn't they be? When you can see the immediate impact of your efforts with your own eyes, it is very exciting indeed.

So the question becomes the most important question... what does YOUR town need? Even in the most affluent place, there is homelessness, hopelessness, poverty, crisis and needs of all kinds from education to civic reform and everything between.

It's time to think...

- What can YOU do?
- Do you have a particular talent or background that you can use here?
- What clever idea can you come up with to solve the problems closest to you?

- Is there an innovative way to solve the problem?
- If you had only $100, what would you do to solve the problem?
- If you had ten other people to help you, what could you do then?
- What could you do with donations of time, effort and supplies, if not money?
- What would success look like?

Now you see the true nature of charity. It is about focusing on the needs of others, thereby feeling how we are larger than just ourselves. And that has nothing to do with money.

# Conclusion

We have seen the nature and effect of money on you, as an individual, over the course of your life and as your wealth grows. We have seen the nature and effect of money on your relationships with your friends, parents and children. And we have seen the nature and effect of government money, other people's money and your own money and time on the world and humanity at large.

Throughout this exploration, there were questions that hopefully brought you closer to understanding your relationship with money and how you use it. There is no right way. There is only the right way for you, as an individual. So here's to your future with your money. May it be a happy and prosperous one!

# Support For Your Journey

# Questions, Answers And Additional Resources

Do you have questions about what you have read here? Go to KathrynColleen.com and send in your questions. Kathryn will answer you back as quickly as possible and may include your question on the podcast or blog.

Also at KathrynColleen.com, you will find:

- Links to the full edition of the book, *Purna Asatti*, which includes specific exercises and how-to for each task plus art and poetry for a different perspective on each stage of your personal development.
- The podcast, *On Life And Being Human*, where many of your questions may be answered.
- Other books, albums, guided meditations, essays and art by Kathryn Colleen.
- And more!

# About The Author

Dr. Amy "Kathryn Colleen" Messegee, PhD RMT is an American-born author, composer and artist better known for her foundational work: *Purna Asatti*, a process and practice that uses connection to self, others and every aspect of your life for managing challenges and accelerating self development.

Her summer job at 16 was doing scientific research at NASA. Before her 25th birthday she earned her PhD in Mathematics and was speaking to conferences on human reasoning and how to make the infinite finite. A hyper-polymath, her career has enjoyed a ride through...

- academia (as a professor of Mathematics),
- defense technology (as a Scientist, CTO, and DARPA Program Manager),
- online media (as founder of a business website and video podcast with a reach of 1.3 million),

- venture capital (advising VC firms on evaluating technologies and reading the founders for their true intent),
- private education (as founder of a local network of elite tutors and private instructors),
- and her current passion: global peace, human connection and energy work.

In each of these, the theme is always the same: aggregating seemingly unrelated perspectives to distill a new approach for accelerated results. She has published many books, hundreds of articles and papers, dozens of unique art pieces and released multiple music albums.

She is known for taking only four students each year but influences and leads thousands around the world in more than 70 countries through speaking, writing, music, art and podcasts.

She is a Reiki Master Practitioner/Teacher and is travel-proficient in nine languages which she is learning simultaneously while living out her dream of traveling the world, speaking at pop up events and aggregating insight on life, the universe and being human.

See KathrynColleen.com for more information, books, articles, music, podcasts, and resources.

www.ingramcontent.com/pod-product-compliance
Lightning Source LLC
LaVergne TN
LVHW010613100826
845148LV00014B/2945

* 9 7 8 1 7 3 5 6 9 4 3 0 6 *